DAVID N. CAMAIONE is Assistant Professor of Physical Education, Coordinator of Men's Physical Education, Assistant Director of Athletics, and Wrestling Coach at Mac-Murray College. As an undergraduate at The Ohio State University, Coach Camaione was Big Ten Champion (123 pounds), and was voted Outstanding Wrestler of the Western Conference Tournament. He has been Chairman of the NAIA District 20 Wrestling Advisory Committee (Illinois), Treasurer of the College Division of the NCAA Wrestling Coaches Association, and was named Wrestling Coach-of-the-Year (1966) in the NAIA District 20.

KENNETH G. TILLMAN, Ph.D., University of New Mexico, is Associate Professor and Chairman of the Men's Physical Education Department, Chairman of the Physical Education Graduate Program, and Wrestling Coach at Southeast Missouri State College. He has previously taught and coached at the University of New Mexico, the University of Illinois, and Augustana College.

WRESTLING
METHODS

David N. Camaione
MacMURRAY COLLEGE

Kenneth G. Tillman
SOUTHEAST MISSOURI STATE COLLEGE

THE RONALD PRESS COMPANY • NEW YORK

Library of Congress Catalog Card Number: 68–13471
PRINTED IN THE UNITED STATES OF AMERICA

To our wives

Judi C.
Delores T.

Preface

This book has been written for both the physical education teacher and the coach. It is especially designed for use in college methods courses for physical education majors studying teaching and coaching techniques. Coaches and teachers in the field also should find the book a useful guide for improving their programs. It will be particularly valuable in school systems which employ a number of teachers for wrestling instruction and are concerned in developing meaningful uniformity and proper progression in course offerings.

The book was written to fill a void which existed in wrestling literature. Although there are many excellent books on wrestling techniques, there are very few which also include the basic principles and fundamentals of administering and conducting a successful wrestling program. This book includes both techniques and methods. In addition, it presents the philosophical considerations for including wrestling in a physical education program, and discusses the values of a well-organized experience in wrestling. The reader is also given a graphic historical analysis of wrestling from its primitive beginnings to its present status in the United States. Practical considerations follow the theoretical discussions. The authors feel that this approach makes the book most valuable.

This book contains what the authors consider to be the basic beginning and advanced wrestling moves currently being used successfully by the outstanding college and high school teams in the United States. It is not the purpose of this textbook to include all possible holds. Sufficient holds are presented to develop successful varsity teams. The main responsibility of the coach is to select the best holds for use in the wrestling program. Additional wrestling maneuvers which are to be found in all of the wrestling technique books listed in the bibliography can be used to supplement moves described in this book.

The authors wish to thank the members of their wrestling teams and wrestling classes for assistance in formulating the ideas and techniques which form the basis for this book. The authors recognize that wrestling procedures are continually being improved. It is hoped that the thoughts and basic procedures presented in this book will give impetus to further growth and improvement of all levels of wrestling in the United States.

DAVID N. CAMAIONE

KENNETH G. TILLMAN

Jacksonville, Illinois
Cape Girardeau, Missouri
   January, 1968

Acknowledgment

The authors wish to express their appreciation to the four wrestlers who demonstrated the maneuvers for the photographs in this book:

Peter Brann, *MacMurray College*
Thomas E. Knight, *MacMurray College*
Walter E. Krahl, III, *Southeast Missouri State College*
William J. Schwab, *Southeast Missouri State College*

Special appreciation is directed to Miss R. Betty Kriegshauser, former Director of Public Relations at MacMurray College, for her efforts in editing the manuscript.

D.N.C.
K.G.T.

Contents

PART II.   THEORY OF TEACHING WRESTLING

7   Organizing, Administering, and Evaluating   .   69

8   Beginning Techniques   86

PART III.   THEORY OF COACHING WRESTLING

9   Organization and Administration   .   .   .   149

Part I

ORIENTATION FOR TEACHER AND COACH

1

A Background

PURPOSES

The possibilities have never been better in this country for having a well-rounded physical education program as an integral part of the educational system. The President's Council on Physical Fitness has dramatically pointed up the need for developing the physical well-being of young people, and has given considerable support in encouraging the public to insist that local schools improve their physical education programs.

With this support, the physical education teacher has the opportunity as never before to make a contribution to the field of education. He has also a responsibility. He must be committed to the building of a program that answers the physical needs of young people and supports and furthers the over-all objectives of his country's educational goals as well as those of the school he serves.

Wrestling, perhaps more than most individual and team sports, helps in physical development and body conditioning. In becoming proficient in the sport, the individual discovers the muscular functions of the human body, and he learns how to use his body efficiently with coordination and poise. Learning the capabilities and limits of the human body is no small accomplishment. And the teacher who achieves this among his students is making a major contribution to the educational effort.

The competitive spirit of wrestling has carry-over values and can help answer the psychological needs of students. The wrestling mat provides a constructive outlet for the pent-up energies, feelings of hostility, and frustration that are symptomatic of today's restless and uncertain teen-ager. And when a young wrestler has to face his opponent, he gains first-hand experience in coping with stresses and pressures that are not unlike those that will confront him throughout his life.

The development of self-discipline is another value and reason for including wrestling in a physical education program. A wrestler is often required to follow a rigid diet. He must become involved in a vigorous program of conditioning. He must learn to follow the rules of the game and conform to standards and policies set by the coach.

In addition to the individual benefits, there are administrative values to the school and its physical education program. Wrestling adds to the variety of course offerings and can strengthen weak physical education programs. Too many programs stagnate through lack of diversification. In some schools, for example, the fall sport is football, basketball is played in the winter, and softball in the spring. This pattern is followed year after year. Wrestling can offer an exciting change in the routine.

In addition to diversifying the program, wrestling is a sport which can be adapted to all age levels. This is accomplished by increasing the complexity of the maneuvers and skills from one grade level to another. Each season, or unit, can be a new experience for the participants. And it can be as challenging to a senior with several seasons behind him as it can be for the sixth or seventh grader who is wrestling for the first time.

For the school administrator concerned with budget, facilities, and burgeoning enrollments, wrestling has a special appeal. Equipment costs are relatively low, and the program can be conducted in the existing gym without major structural changes. Or, at little cost, some unused area in the school plant can be adapted to wrestling and still serve as well for another teaching station.

The purposes and values of wrestling for the school's physical education program apply also for the varsity athletic program. Obviously, varsity wrestling offers a greater opportunity for increased participation in the over-all athletic program. But it has special advantages, too; many students unable to compete in the usual varsity sports can often make the wrestling team because size and body build are no restrictions.

Wrestling, as a part of the physical education program or varsity athletic program, is compatible with the purposes of education. Under dedicated leadership, it can provide an opportunity for each participating student to grow mentally and emotionally, as well as physically.

VALUES

Wrestling is considered by many to be America's fastest growing sport. Its phenomenal growth over the last fifteen years has occurred primarily in our high schools and colleges. Until this recent upsurge of popularity, wrestling was found only in limited areas scattered throughout the country. Today, it is spreading rapidly in almost every state.

Wrestling is expanding also into new age groups. Whereas once the sport was concentrated in high schools and colleges, there is now "kid wrestling" for boys between the ages of four and twelve, junior high school wrestling has increased, and wrestling clubs for boys and men alike are on the incline.

The values of wrestling help explain its popularity. Any boy, regardless of size, has an opportunity to compete successfully because competition is classed by weight, and the weight difference between wrestlers is never more than a few pounds. As a result, wrestling is one of the few sports not dominated by those who have some specific advantage, such as size.

Many schools feel that the greatest advantage of a wrestling program is that smaller boys can take part in a varsity sport and gain the sportsmanship values inherent in all competitive sports. Also, boys of varying body builds can become skillful wrestlers. Some styles, for example, are better suited to the tall, thin boy. Yet, the short, stocky boy can be equally as successful by using different wrestling maneuvers.

Wrestling is one of the best sports for developing physical fitness. This potential value of the sport doubtless accounts for the increased interest among schools and colleges for including wrestling in their regular physical education programs. Because wrestling brings every muscle into play, it develops physical stature, builds body tonus, increases cardio-vascular efficiency, improves balance, and develops quickness, agility, flexibility, and power. It helps the boy to overcome his awkwardness and develop poise and physical efficiency.

Wrestling can contribute to the development of personality characteristics and encourage the qualities that are important in the development of a well-rounded, mature person. A student participating in wrestling naturally learns such traits as courage, determination, and initiative. A wrestler, "on his own" on the mat, soon learns to be aggressive in a healthy way, and acquires self-confidence and self-reliance.

Another value of wrestling, which should not be overlooked, is the art of self-defense. Boys or men with wrestling skills and a knowledge of leverage, body position and balance, are better equipped to cope intelligently and effectively with physical dangers which may threaten their lives or the life and safety of another person in peril.

There are few sports in which a contestant is as completely on his own as when a wrestler steps forward and makes physical contact with his opponent. This demands tremendous courage. A wrestler knows that his performance depends upon himself, how well he has mastered the techniques and how well he applies them. Out of these stringent demands on the individual come perhaps the greatest rewards of wrestling.

One of wrestling's unique values is that it is a sport in which the severely handicapped can participate and even become competent. Blind boys become very proficient wrestlers. Many schools for the handicapped teach wrestling and conduct their own regional tournaments.

Wrestling is also growing as a recreational sport. The Y.M.C.A. and many clubs are providing wrestling facilities where all ages can participate. Wrestling lends itself to this type of activity since it takes only two to get an enjoyable workout with a minimum amount of equipment. The severity and length of the workout can be easily controlled. It is possible to receive maximum benefit in a very short period of time if "full go" wrestling is desired. By slowing down the tempo it is possible to extend the length of time the wrestlers can enjoy wrestling without becoming overly fatigued. Another important factor is that men of different age groups can enjoy wrestling against each other. The older, more experienced wrestler can compete recreationally with the younger man because of his greater competency in executing the wrestling moves.

Every boy has an innate desire to engage in rough and tumble activity with his peers. Knowledge of wrestling makes it possible for boys to satisfy this youthful urge and to continue to receive the benefits of this activity in their adult years.

Opportunities for developing social competencies are evident in wrestling. A wrestler learns to respect the talents and abilities of others. He learns to obey the rules of the sport and to accept the judgment of officials. Even though he is alone when wrestling, he soon learns the importance of team unity and cooperation with his teammates, and coordinates his own desires with others for the good of the team. In the competitive situation a wrestler learns to control his emotions and treat opponents with respect.

BRIEF HISTORY

Wrestling is one of the oldest sporting activities. Its development can be traced back to primitive man. Since early man had no weapons, he had to learn hand-to-hand combat techniques not only to battle the wild beasts, but also to struggle against man's worst enemy, man himself. As time went on and certain tools of defense were developed, wrestling became less important as a means of survival. Man, however, continued in the art of hand-to-hand fighting to satisfy his natural urge to engage a fellow man in combat. This change of emphasis probably established wrestling as an activity for sporting purposes. Ancient records document the presence of the art of wrestling. Art works depicting hand-to-hand combat have been found upon the walls of the temple-tomb of Beni Hasan along the river Nile. The early cultures of the Babylonians, Egyptians, and Hindus used wrestling as an educational tool to instruct their young in offensive techniques for battle.

Greece gave added rigidity and sophistication to the art of wrestling. According to one Greek myth, Zeus acquired possession of the earth by defeating Kronos in a wrestling match along the river Alphus at Olympia in 776 B.C. Historians believe that the commemoration of this battle gave rise to the ancient Olympic Games. Wrestling was later an important part of the Pentathlon event of the ancient games. The Pentathlon demonstrated all-around athletic ability by involving the athlete in the rigorous tasks of running, jumping, throwing the discus and javelin, and wrestling. The Greeks probably made the greatest contribution to wrestling when in 704 B.C. they introduced it as a major sport in the Olympic Games, because they held the wrestler in high esteem, second only to the discus thrower.

With the fall of Greece to Roman conquest, two new styles of wrestling evolved. The Greco-Roman style differed only slightly from the original Grecian style and continued to restrict the use of holds below the waist. The pragmatic Romans developed free-style wrestling where all holds were accepted. Their militant influence demanded that every sport must have as its ultimate objective the development of skills for military warfare. Both the Greco-Roman and free-style forms of wrestling have changed little through the ages. It is interesting to note that these are the only styles used in today's international competition and in the modern Olympic Games.

Around the 16th century, many styles of wrestling were in vogue in Europe and specifically in England. In the 19th Century, three prominent forms were added to the Greek and Roman influences, giving us our modern forms of free-style wrestling. The Lancashire style, which gave rise to the catch-as-catch-can style, required holding the opponent's shoulders to the ground for a period of two seconds. The Cumberland or Westmoreland style differed from the Lancashire in that wrestling on the ground was the fundamental aspect of the form. The Devon or Cornish style employed techniques to throw an opponent to the ground.

There also have been many forms of wrestling throughout the Orient. Some believe that the ancient art of hand wrestling may have had its beginning 5,000 years ago in India. There are four forms of wrestling known to have had their origins in the Orient: Sumo, Judo, Karate, and Aikido. Sumo, probably one of the oldest forms, has as its objective the throwing of an opponent off balance so that any part of his body will touch the ground. Judo, a type of personal defense which has evolved into a sport using throws and controlling mat holds, traces back to the 12th century technique of Jiujitsu. Judo was installed in the XVIII Olympiad in Tokyo to honor the host of the games, the Japanese people. Karate, once the art of killing with a single blow, is the third well-known technique, which most historians feel originated in Okinawa around the 17th century. It has, however, more recently become one of the popular sporting arts in many countries. The fourth style, known as Aikido, is a recent development having its origin in the 20th century. It is also a skill of self-defense mainly concerned with disarming an opponent or enemy by the use of parrying tactics.

WRESTLING IN THE UNITED STATES

The American Indians used wrestling as a tool of self-defense against enemy tribes and as a sporting event at festivals long before Columbus set foot on the continent. The earliest settlers of the colonies brought hand-to-hand combat wrestling with them. Probably the best known of the early American wrestlers is Abraham Lincoln, who fought in matches in New Salem, Illinois, and in nearby villages.

The revival of the modern Olympic Games by Baron Pierre de Coubertin of France gave wrestling an opportunity to receive world-wide acclaim when it became an official part of the program of the III Olympiad, held in St. Louis, Missouri, in 1904.

The first intercollegiate dual match took place in 1900 between the University of Pennsylvania and Yale University. Its apparent success spread so rapidly throughout the East that in 1904 the Eastern Intercollegiate Wrestling Conference was formed to set up an established system of rules to govern competition. In 1927 the NCAA organized the Wrestling Rules Committee to attempt to standardize a set of rules and to regulate the policies and procedures of wrestling competition. This was one of the giant steps taken in popularizing wrestling throughout the United States. The NCAA annually holds its championships to further promote the values of wrestling. Almost from the inception of the tournament, the Big Eight Conference teams of Oklahoma State (former Oklahoma A&M), University of Oklahoma, and Iowa State University have heavily dominated its proceedings.

Catch-as-catch-can is the style used at the interscholastic and intercollegiate level. The "rolling pin" was once the main difference between international freestyle and catch-as-catch-can wrestling; however, recent changes in this ruling have brought the two together so that the terms may now be used interchangeably. Each demands proficiency on the feet, each demands skill enabling one to control another in the offensive position, and each demands that the wrestler work toward the ultimate objective, the fall.

THE FUTURE OF WRESTLING

Wrestling in the United States is flourishing at all levels of competition. It is constantly undergoing change. The rules and regulations are annually reviewed in an attempt to arrive at the best possible set of standards for the participant in particular, and in general for the spectator.

The international style of wrestling has greatly influenced our thinking about the present day form predominately used in the United States. However, only in AAU tournaments do the two forms of free-style and Greco-Roman make their appearance in America. An ever-growing number of such wrestling groups as Y.M.C.A. teams, athletic clubs, and service teams demonstrate the need to examine the possibilities of making additional provisions to foster more competition under international rules, so that all American wrestlers might be better prepared to compete on the international scene. A newly-formed United States Wrestling Federation is attempting to make progress toward this goal by sponsoring wrestling for the many groups in the United States to the end that the properly selected and trained participant becomes the sole benefactor.

Wrestling will continue to grow because of the improved techniques of training and coaching, better equipment and facilities, and outstanding enthusiasm on the part of many dedicated individuals who are working toward the best interests of the sport.

Additional historical information can be obtained from many of the references noted in the bibliography.

2

Rules and Competition

OFFICIAL RULES

The official rules governing collegiate and scholastic wrestling are established by the NCAA Wrestling Rules Committee and printed in the *Official Wrestling Guide,* published annually by the National Collegiate Athletic Bureau. Following are brief descriptions of the rules, in the format of the wrestling guide.[1]

RULE I—ELIGIBILITY

All participants shall be amateurs and eligible according to the regulations of the institution (scholastic or collegiate) which he represents.

RULE II—REPRESENTATION

Each member institution may be represented by only one contestant in each weight.

RULE III—MATS, COSTUMES, EQUIPMENT

Mats. The wrestling area shall not be less than 24 feet by 24 feet square or a circular area of 28 feet in diameter. A mat of at least 5 feet in width shall extend around the wrestling area. A circle 10 feet in diameter shall be placed in the middle of the mat.

Costume. College ruling requires full length tights, overtights, and sleeveless shirts. The high school ruling will vary according to the prerogative of the individual states.

Equipment. Equipment requirements will be discussed in Chapter 7.

---

[1] Permission to use the preceding material from the *Official Wrestling Guide* was granted by the National Collegiate Athletic Bureau.

Rule IV—Weight Classifications

Intercollegiate classifications are 123, 130, 137, 145, 152, 160, 167, 177, and heavyweight. The 115 and 191 divisions may be included in dual meets and are required in NCAA championship tournaments.

Interscholastic classifications are 103, 112, 120, 127, 133, 138, 145, 154, 165, and heavyweight. The 95 and 180 pound divisions may be officially included.[2]

Rule V—Weighing-in Procedures

Tournaments. The contestant must weigh in each day of the tournament with an additional pound allowance for each day of competition.

Dual Meets. The contestants may weigh in a maximum of five hours and minimum of one-half hour before the schedule time. The interscholastic ruling varies; in the majority of the states, a contestant may weigh in a maximum of one hour and a minimum of one-half hour before the time of the meet.

Rule VI—Conduct of Tournaments

In all tournaments four places shall be awarded, except in national championship meets when six are awarded. Drawings and seeding of top competitors may be administered by a group of competing coaches or by a previously selected committee.

The Bagnall-Wild tournament is commonly used in wrestling. Each wrestler defeated by an ultimate finalist in his weight class wrestles back in a single elimination tournament to determine the third and fourth place finishers. When there are a large number of entries and the tournament has to be run off in limited time, a single elimination tournament is used.

Rule VII—Conduct of Matches

Intercollegiate. All regular matches shall be eight minutes in length, 2–3–3. The match is started with the wrestlers in the neutral position. The second and third periods begin with the wrestlers assuming the referee's position. In tournaments when the regular match ends in a draw, three one-minute periods shall be added. Consolation matches

[2] Some state high school athletic associations include weight classifications in addition to, or varying from, the twelve classifications specified by the NCAA. The exact classifications of a given state can be obtained from the high school athletic organization in that state.

CHAMPIONSHIP BRACKET

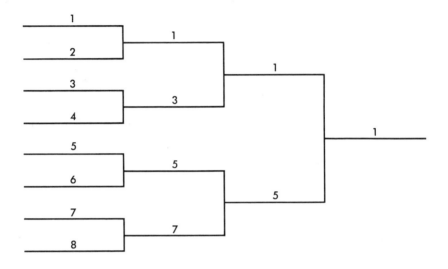

CONSOLATION BRACKET

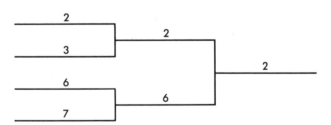

Fig. 2–1. Bagnall-Wild Tournament Bracketing

shall consist of three two-minute periods, with three one-minute over-time periods for tied bouts.

Interscholastic. All regular matches shall consist of three two-minute periods. In tournaments, when the regular match ends in a draw, two one-minute periods shall be added.

RULE VIII—DEFINITIONS

This material is covered in the Glossary at the end of the book.

RULE IX—SCORING SYSTEMS

Individual Match Scoring

Takedown	2 points
Escape	1 point
Reversal	2 points
Near-fall	3 points
Predicament	2 points
Time Advantage	Maximum of 2 points

Dual Meet Team Scoring

Fall	5 points
Decision	3 points
Draw	2 points
Forfeit	5 points
Default	5 points

Tournament Scoring (See *Official Wrestling Guide* for scoring when six places are awarded)

First Place	10 points
Second Place	7 points
Third Place	4 points
Fourth Place	2 points
Fall	1 point
Advancement	1 point
Forfeit	1 point
Default	1 point
Disqualification	1 point

RULE X—INFRACTIONS

Illegal Holds, Intercollegiate

Hammerlock above the right angle
Twisting hammerlock
Front headlock
Straight head scissors
Flying mare with palm up
Full-nelson
Strangle holds
All body slams
Toe holds
Twisting knee lock
Key lock
Overhead double bar-arm
All headlocks without the arm or leg

Note: Any hold may be construed as illegal if it becomes dangerous to the life or limb of the contestant.

Technical Violations

Interlocking hands
Leaving mat without permission
Delaying match
Intentionally forcing opponent off mat
Intentionally going off mat, any position
Grasping of clothes
Stalling, any position

RULE XI—PENALTIES

Infractions to the rules are judged according to prearranged procedure listed on a Penalty Chart, which is too complicated to give in this text.

Note: Check bibliography for listing of *Official Wrestling Guide*.

The referee at the time of an infraction shall stop the match, give the proper hand signal, and award the penalty point(s) to the contestant.

RULE XII—INJURIES AND DEFAULTS

Injuries. An injured contestant is allowed three minutes of injury time throughout the regular match and overtime. Injuries involving excessive bleeding have unlimited time-out's.

Defaults. If a contestant is accidentally injured and is unable to continue, the match is awarded to his opponent. If the injury was due to an illegal action, and the contestant is unable to continue, the match is awarded to the injured participant.

RULE XIII—OFFICIALS

The official is the sole judge and interpreter of all rules and regulations concerning the overall conduct of a meet or tournament.

FORMS OF COMPETITION

Many types of wrestling are in vogue today. The teacher or coach, therefore, should be equipped to select, organize and administer the forms which fit his situation. The more popular forms are described here.

The dual meet is the most popular, because it poses the "head-to-head" battle of squads. The face-to-face contact in a dual meet makes the sport challenging and exciting.

Invitational tournaments with five or more teams competing give the wrestler valuable experience in preparing for conference meets or state qualifying rounds.

Double-duals, triangulars, or triple-dual combinations allow teams to compete against several opponents on the same day, thereby saving expense and travel time.

The quadrangular set-up gives the team an opportunity to experience brief tournament competition by providing two matches for each contestant. This form is administered with two rounds. The four coaches decide in advance of the meet which two wrestlers in each weight class are to be seeded. The second round pits the winners of each bracket against each other for first and second place. Losers of the first round compete for third and fourth place.

If seeding is not appropriate, the following procedure may be used to determine opponents. Each team draws for a number. The numbers are then paired and set up in a round-robin fashion.

FIRST WEIGHT CLASS: 1 vs 2, 3 vs 4.
SECOND WEIGHT CLASS: 1 vs 3, 2 vs 4.
THIRD WEIGHT CLASS: 1 vs 4, 2 vs 3.

Dual Meets

Teams compete against each other in dual meets. Both teams have a representative in each weight classification. The winning wrestler gains three points for his team if he wins by a decision, five points if he pins his opponent. A tie gives each team two points. A pin, or fall, is awarded if a wrestler holds the shoulders or scapula areas of his opponent in contact with the mat for one second; two seconds in interscholastic wrestling. If there is no fall, the winner is determined by the number of points earned during the course of the match. Disqualifications, forfeits, and defaults also give five points to the team score.

Quadrangulars and Tournaments

In quadrangulars and tournaments, team-scoring is based on place points, 10, 7, 4, and 2, respectively, for first, second, third, and fourth places in each weight class. Each wrestler receives one additional team point for a pin (fall), default, forfeit, or disqualification, and a point for every time he advances in the tournament. He gets this advancement point for every match he wins except for the final championship or consolation match.

Double-Duals or Triangular

Three teams compete in this type of wrestling. Three scores are kept for each team. One is the score of the triangular meet; two scores are dual meet scores against the other teams. The triangular meet is scored 5–3–1 for each weight class. If the wrestlers end with identical records, each team is awarded three points.

Pairings for triangular meets can be:

FIRST WEIGHT CLASS: 1 vs 2, 2 vs 3, 1 vs 3.
SECOND WEIGHT CLASS: 1 vs 3, 1 vs 2, 2 vs 3.
THIRD WEIGHT CLASS: 2 vs 3, 1 vs 3, 1 vs 2.

Two possible finishes in a triangular meet are:

2 wins, 0 losses, 5 team points
1 win, 1 loss, 3 team points
0 win, 2 losses, 1 team point

and

1 win, 1 loss, 3 team points
1 win, 1 loss, 3 team points
1 win, 1 loss, 3 team points

Triple-Dual Meets

Triple-dual meets rather than quadrangulars are recent innovations in wrestling competition. Four teams meet in three sessions during the day. Each team wrestles three dual meets rather than in a four-team quadrangular tournament.

The system for selection of numbers for each team is the same as discussed under quadrangulars.

FIRST ROUND: 1 vs 2, 3 vs 4.
SECOND ROUND: 1 vs 3, 2 vs 4.
THIRD ROUND: 1 vs 4, 2 vs 3.

International Competition

International competition utilizes a different kind of tournament. Wrestlers are paired according to a drawing held prior to competition. Pairing with a different opponent continues until there are only three contestants remaining with less than six penalty points. These contestants then wrestle a round robin to determine the winner. The winner is the contestant with the fewest penalty points. If there is a pin, the winner receives no penalty points and the loser, four. The winner of a decision receives one penalty point and the loser, three. Each wrestler receives two penalty points in a draw.

3

Physical Aspects of Wrestling

INJURIES

Wrestling programs must be based on sound organizational principles to prevent injuries. Protective equipment such as head-gear and knee-pads should be used for advanced levels of wrestling. Also, the wrestling area must be free of unpadded obstructions, exposed concrete floor, and unmatted walls directly adjacent to the wrestling mat.

The person who coaches a wrestling team or teaches wrestling classes must use the proper teaching progression and know the correct precautions which will minimize the possibility of injury. Many wrestling programs have failed because the instructor or coach disregarded weight differences, failed to apply sound training methods and warm-up routines, or did not properly teach the difference between a legal and an illegal hold. An even greater failing of the inexperienced teacher is the temptation to start students wrestling before they know basic maneuvers. This type of wrestling frequently develops into a flailing free-for-all that not only discourages the participants, but leads to serious injury. Teaching proper progression of wrestling maneuvers is essential for the welfare of the student and the reception received by the wrestling program. This book explains the proper techniques to follow for teaching and coaching wrestling.

A thorough medical examination should be required for every boy who competes on the wrestling team. A routine medical examination is necessary for all students who participate in instructional, intramural, and interscholastic wrestling programs. Most high schools and colleges make provisions for periodic health examinations of all their students. Directors of physical education and athletics should strongly recommend this procedure.

A boy should never wrestle with gum or food in his mouth. Naturally, pep pills and similar stimulants can never be used. Rings and similar devices are dangerous to both the contestant and his opponent and are not permitted by the rules. Uniforms for team and class use must be free of metal parts and other foreign substances which might injure the participant.

In spite of all precautions, some injuries will occur due to the contact nature of the sport. Therefore, it is important to know and to use the proper treatment which will minimize the seriousness of an injury and hasten the wrestler's recovery.

EMERGENCY CARE

When an injury occurs, the first principle to follow is to accurately evaluate the extent of the injury. If the wrestler becomes unconscious, a doctor should be consulted before he is permitted to wrestle again. When a fracture or separation is suspected or a dislocation is present, the involved area should be immobilized, and the wrestler taken to the trainer or doctor. Medical advice should be obtained whenever there is doubt about the severity of an injury.

Since relatively few serious injuries occur in wrestling, the coach or teacher will primarily need basic knowledge of the proper treatment for the injuries described below.

Matburn. With the advent of the cellular rubber wrestling mat, this injury has become infrequent. It is a form of an abrasion involving the scraping off of the outer layers of the skin. Infection is the primary danger. The injured area should be thoroughly cleansed with soap and water. After cleaning, an approved antiseptic should be applied. A dressing may be necessary to prevent further aggravation. An ointment dressing should be used if the matburn is located on a joint. Otherwise, it is best to let the affected area heal naturally.

Sprains.   A sprain is a joint twist that results in stretching or tearing stabilizing connective tissues. Treatment should consist of immediate application of an elastic bandage compress and ice. Pressure and cold should be applied intermittently during a period of 24 to 48 hours. The length of time will depend on the severity of the injury. Later, heat and whirlpool treatment will help speed recovery. The injured part should be taped until the connective tissue has healed. *

Strain.   A strain is a tear to the muscle or surrounding tissue. A compression bandage and ice pack should be applied immediately to reduce swelling. This is followed by heat treatment and sufficient rest to allow the injured part to heal.

Muscular Contusions.   This type of injury is a bruise resulting from a blow to the muscle. Internal hemorrhaging will occur, so immediate application of compression bandages and ice is important to stop the bleeding. Treatment is similar to a sprain in that after 48 hours, heat should be applied.

Lacerations and Incised Wounds.   Any time the skin is broken, the injured area should be carefully washed and an antiseptic applied to the wound. A bandage of some type might be necessary to protect the injury while healing. Consult the doctor or trainer if the wound is large enough to possibly warrant stitches.

Nose Bleed.   Have the wrestler lie down with neck hyperextended. Apply a cold pack to nape of neck and over bridge of nose and eyes. Pressure on the upper lip or the bridge of the nose may also stop bleeding. Gauze or cotton plugs in the nostrils will give pressure and aid in stopping bleeding.

Impetigo.   Impetigo is an infectious disease of the outer layers of the skin. It is highly communicable and can therefore cause problems for the wrestling teacher or coach. Streptococci and staphylococci will pass from wrestler to wrestler when the pus and serum present in the infection on one wrestler come into contact with a break in the skin of another wrestler. Proper

---

*Ice therapy together with exercise is another treatment technique being used extensively for sprains, strains, and contusions.

sanitation is essential to prevent impetigo. The wrestling mat and mat area should be frequently mopped with a disinfectant. If a wrestler has impetigo, he must be isolated immediately. The scabs should be removed and an application of an ointment such as sulfathiazole, gentian violet, phemerol, ammoniated mercury, or penicillin applied. The rest of the group should soap and shower, then wash with alcohol.

Cauliflower Ear.   Headgear will prevent a cauliflower ear from developing. Treatment consists of aspiration and application of a collodion pack. This should be done only by a physician. Care should be taken to prevent infection.

Boils.   Boils are infections resulting when staphylococci enter the body through a break in the skin. These infections sometimes occur in wrestling when proper personal and mat cleanliness have not been maintained. They are likely to develop around a hair follicle. Treatment consists of periodic soaking with hot packs to draw the boil to a head and application of an antibiotic ointment to the area. The core of the boil should be allowed to come out naturally. Further steps in treating a boil should be carried out by a qualified trainer or physician. It is essential that uniforms, mats, and the body of the wrestler be thoroughly cleaned after every practice to prevent boils from developing. If a wrestler does have a boil, extreme care in personal and mat cleanliness must be exercised to prevent boils from spreading to other parts of his body and to other wrestlers. Again, washing with alcohol by all participants will help stop the spread of the germ.

WEIGHT CONTROL

Excessive weight reduction is the number one criticism of amateur wrestling, and one of the major reasons why it is difficult to justify wrestling for some athletic programs. There are programs which require the wrestler to make *excessive* weight drops throughout the season. This may cause harm to the normal growth cycle of an adolescent, although research in the field is not conclusive on this point. However, properly controlled weight reduction over a long period of time has not been found to have deleterious effects on the growth of adolescents. In the main, programs that have sophisticated control of weight reduction by trained personnel far out-number those with false standards.

Dedicated leaders in the sport have made great strides in correcting the problem of weight reduction. Recent rule changes in the number of weight classes and their systematic spacing based upon national norm findings is an example of the way the problem is being solved. Many states have set up individual standards allowing for one weigh-in at the beginning of the year with designated spot certification checks during the season. Some have a five pound allowance between the certification dates for scheduled matches. This is one sample of the many experimental programs now being used in an attempt to alleviate this constant problem of weight reduction that plagues our sport.

The purpose of this section is to outline a few general considerations for the coach conducting a weight control program.

1. Encourage the wrestlers to eat well-balanced meals including meat, vegetables, milk, bread, and fruit to ensure proper eating habits.
2. It is best for the wrestler to eat the regular three meals a day; however, if some meal must be forfeited for dieting, emphasize the importance that it be other than breakfast.
3. It is recommended that liquid nutrition such as Hustle, Top Star, and Nutrament be used by the wrestler, because of their nutritional value and ease in digestion.
4. It is recommended that multiple vitamin pills and vitamin C tablets be distributed to the wrestlers to prevent deficiencies.
5. Be aware of too great a loss of salt content as well as water. Periodic use of salt pills is recommended.
6. Once the wrestler has "weighed in," it is important for him to take substantial amounts of water to replenish water lost during weight reduction.
7. The wrestler should be cautioned not to eat large amounts of fats during the pre-match meal, because of the difficulty in breaking down the fat molecule during digestion.
8. A diet rich in carbohydrates is recommended for the pre-match meal.

9. Suggested pre-match meal (five hours before the contest).

Orange juice	Baked potato
Fruit cup	Toasted bread
Hot tea	Sherbet
Steak (filet) 8 ounces	Honey
Green beans	Water

Some coaches and wrestlers desire a lighter meal after weighing in. This is particularly true if less than five hours before the match. Alternate pre-match meals are:

a. Orange juice
   Two poached eggs
   Toasted bread
   Honey
   Hot tea
   Water

b. Liquid nutrition (particularly good for the wrestler who is nervous and has difficulty digesting a solid meal)

Gradual weight reduction during the week of "making weight" is the best method to be employed. Lessening the food intake first and then the water intake will ensure the best results. Suggested weight reduction plan for 145-pound wrestler:

Monday	150.5	pounds after practice.
Tuesday	149	pounds after practice.
Wednesday	148.5	pounds after practice.
Thursday	147	pounds after practice.
Friday	145	pounds after practice.
Saturday	145	pounds at the weigh-in.

The use of artificial devices by which a wrestler may lose weight has been highly criticized by medical authorities. The whirlpool, sweatbox, and similar devices have been ruled illegal by the high school law-making group. This is an excellent innovation. Far too many coaches in the past have allowed their wrestlers to subject themselves to long hours using these devices. Proper diet procedures make these methods unnecessary. If the coach is alert to the weight of each wrestler, much of this can be avoided or completely eliminated. This is one of the main reasons why there should be a weight chart kept either in the wrestling room area or the locker room area.

The authors, again, wish to emphasize the need for gradual weight reduction and have listed important points which the coach may give to the wrestler:

1. Eliminate eating between meals.

2. Stay away from "junk foods" such as pastries, nuts, candies, and the like.
3. Lessen the intake of potatoes, bread, peas, and corn.
4. Eat little butter or margarine.
5. Avoid creamed vegetables.
6. Increase the consumption of green, leafy vegetables, fish, cottage cheese, and jello.
7. Take in fruits low in calories such as oranges rather than bananas.
8. Eat poultry and eggs.
9. Eat cereals at the breakfast meal.
10. Drink fruit juices rather than carbonated beverages.

4

Facilities and Equipment

BASIC ESSENTIALS FOR ADEQUATE FACILITIES

Almost any place, reasonable in size and without obstructions, can be used as a teaching area for wrestling. Balconies of gymnasiums, a small classroom, even a storage area can be used as practice areas.

Here are some guidelines a coach may find useful in preparing a statement to the administration on the minimum requirements needed to run a first-class program:

1. Floor space should be available for at least two 24' by 24' wrestling mats.
2. Walls should be padded and obstructions removed or covered with padding to prevent injuries.
3. It is best that there be controlled heating units. However, it is suggested that the temperature not exceed 88–90°. In addition, there should be exhaust fans if the room is enclosed.
4. The lighting should be both natural and artificial, if at all possible.
5. The room or wrestling area should be kept clean. The mats should be cleaned at least twice a day, preferably just prior to the first class period and again before practice begins.
6. The wrestling area should be easily accessible to the training room and to the main floor where the mats must be moved for meets.
7. The room should be painted with pastel colors to give a brighter atmosphere.

There are numerous other ideas that the resourceful coach or teacher can bring to focus. These are mentioned in more detail in Chapter 9.

EQUIPMENT REQUIREMENTS

Basic Essentials

Wrestling does not require an extensive amount of equipment. Almost any type of gym uniform can be used for non-competitive wrestling; specific recommendations for physical education uniforms and uniform requirements for interscholastic and intercollegiate meets are discussed later in the chapter. The major piece of equipment is a good wrestling mat. Tying gymnastic mat strips together to form a wrestling mat cannot be defended either from the standpoint of performance or safety. The only mat that a school should consider purchasing is the cellular rubber wrestling mat. The long range economy and continued high performance of the mat over a period of years makes it the best buy.

The development of cellular rubber wrestling mats during the past ten years has provided an unparalleled impetus to wrestling. These mats are rapidly replacing the two-inch hair felt mat which meets the minimum standard required for competitive wrestling. Disadvantages of hair felt mats are: one, they require plastic mat covers which are difficult to keep in place without wrinkling, and two, their interiors have a tendency to pack together. After a period of use they do not provide adequate protection.

The cellular mat is light enough to move easily and can be kept clean with minimum care. It provides a perfect wrestling surface and its resiliency provides maximum protection for the wrestler. This mat has been found to retain its resiliency over a period of years even with extensive use. Another important advantage is that it can be purchased in sections to fit into different shaped areas or into space too small to hold a regular size wrestling mat. The sections can be taped together when a wrestling meet is held. The tape will not damage the mat and can be used throughout the entire season.

A regulation size wrestling mat (see Chapter 2) is required for competitive wrestling. However, participants can enjoy wrestling when they have a matted area of sufficient size to permit them to execute moves without danger of coming into contact with obstructions.

The authors recommend that a minimum of 45 square feet of mat surface per wrestler be available for optimum teaching conditions. The area should be free of obstructions and have protective mats reaching to a height of five feet on the walls.

Physical Education Equipment

The regular physical education uniform may be used for wrestling classes. Most schools require gym shorts and a heavy cotton shirt with perhaps the school emblem on it. This uniform is satisfactory for wrestling classes, since it provides freedom of movement and is easy to keep clean. Sweat pants and sweat shirts are an alternative uniform.

An athletic supporter and athletic socks should be worn at all times. Class members should be encouraged to wear high-top shoes that tie above the ankle; low cuts are illegal in competition because they frequently come off and cause delays. It will probably be difficult to require all students to have high-top shoes since many will already have low cut shoes and be unable to purchase another pair of shoes for the wrestling class. Except for the delays that will be caused while wrestling, the low cut shoe can be used satisfactorily.

At least two clocks should be available to time the length of drills and matches during a physical education class.

Varsity Equipment

Practice Needs. Each wrestler will need a practice uniform plus high-top wrestling shoes. A basketball type shoe is permissible but a shoe designed specifically for wrestling is lighter and provides better contact with the mat surface. An athletic supporter and athletic socks are also necessary.

Various types of uniforms are worn for practice sessions. The authors' teams have used several different types. On the basis of this experience the following practice uniforms are listed in order of preference.

1. Combination nylon–cotton calf-length tights with reinforced gusset crotch, and combination nylon–cotton tight-fitting half-length sleeved sweat shirts with a reinforced gusset under the arms.
2. Cotton wrestling tights and over-tights with a cotton sweat shirt having three-quarter-length sleeves.
3. Cotton sweat pants and cotton sweat shirt.
4. Cotton shorts and heavy weight cotton T-shirt.

Wrestlers should wear protective knee pads during practice sessions. The 11-inch knee pads curved to fit the contour of the knee are the recommended type since they stay in place and provide full protection.

A headgear is also strongly recommended for all varsity wrestlers during practice sessions. Headgear should fit snugly to the head and form a protective cup over the ears. Frequent pressure exerted directly on the ear surface may result in a cauliflower ear if headgear is not worn.

Other practice items used by most teams are the woven-nylon-coated sweat jacket and sweat pants. They are ideal to wear when a wrestler needs to lose weight.

There should be a wall clock in every practice room. This makes it possible for the coach to properly follow his practice plan.

Several timers should be available to time wrestle-offs and wrestling drills used during practice. Some teams use a central timer which can be set for varying lengths of time by the manager. This type of a timer presents an audible signal when the time allotted for a period of wrestling or drilling is completed.

An innovation currently being used by many of the top wrestling teams is a blinking light placed in a position where it will be visible from any spot in the wrestling room. Wrestlers can use this as a starting signal rather than wait for a command from the coach or a teammate.

Competition Needs. For the varsity meet, the uniform should fit well and be distinctive, attractive, easily cleaned, and durable. Stretch nylon is being used successfully by many wrestling teams. Wrestling rules require that long tights, overtights, and a sleeveless jersey be worn by all contestants (see Chapter 2).

The amount of trim on a uniform is a matter of taste. It is suggested that holding to a minimum of trim and lettering adds to the dignity of the sport.

Warm-up pants and shirts contribute to the appearance of the varsity team. Washable materials such as nylon and orlon fleece are attractive and are easily cleaned. The amount of trim and lettering varies according to the wishes of the team and coach.

Some teams use colored knee pads and headgear for their varsity meets. If a team has sufficient funds, this added touch contributes to team morale. Otherwise, headgear and knee pads used during practice can be used for the varsity meets.

An athletic supporter, athletic socks, and light-weight wrestling shoes are also needed for the varsity performer during a meet.

A traveling bag should be available for each contestant. The bag should be large enough to hold all traveling equipment and fold up for easy storage when not in use. Canvas bags wear well and can be obtained in school colors.

In addition to individual equipment, other items are needed during the wrestling meet. Unless the wrestling mat is regulation size, pressure-sensitive tape is needed to tape the mat pieces together to form a regulation wrestling mat.

A large, clearly visible clock is needed to keep the time of each match and the individual match scores during the meet. A separate scoreboard should be available for keeping the team scores.

Riding-time clocks must be provided. Most schools have one clock for the visiting-team wrestler and one for the home-team wrestler. A number of different riding-time clocks are available.

An official scorebook is needed for recording the results of all dual meets. Tournament result sheets are used when the wrestling team participates in a tournament.

A scale which is periodically certified for accuracy is necessary for weigh-in procedures. The scale should be placed in a location where it will be accessible to the wrestlers but will be protected from abuse.

Purchase of Equipment

Only quality equipment should be purchased for a wrestling program. This is advisable from the standpoint of economy, appearance, and safety.

Many sporting goods dealers have a limited experience in wrestler needs. It is, therefore, important to list exact specifications for all wrestling equipment you purchase. Satisfaction can best be obtained by purchasing only from reputable firms. Most of these firms will sell through a local sporting goods store if it is the policy of your school to purchase from local suppliers.

Money can be saved if you request bids on all major items that you purchase. Again, give exact specifications and reserve the right to determine whether bids on a particular item are equal. It is frequently the best policy to pay slightly more for an item that has proven itself through extensive use.

Special caution should be exercised in purchasing a wrestling mat. Many companies are manufacturing this item with insufficient knowledge of the technical aspects of mat manufacturing.

Good equipment records must be kept in order to insure wise equipment purchases. An up-to-date inventory should be available at all times to indicate the amount of equipment on hand and its current condition. This will make it possible to purchase in advance of the season when service is best and better discounts are available. This procedure will help prevent the embarrassment of running short of an item or items during the season.

The following information is an added feature of this book. Buying equipment for any sport is a tedious task. It is hoped that this will be of great benefit to the reader. The companies listed are those agencies which deal in the handling of wrestling equipment in whole or in part.

General Supply for Wrestling

Champion Knitwear Company, Rochester, N.Y. Championship Wrestling Products, Ames, Ia. Cliff Keen Wrestling Products, Ann Arbor, Mich. Olympic Wrestling Products, Valley Stream, L. I., N.Y. Rawlings Sporting Goods Co., St. Louis; New York. Roderick, Incorporated, Garden City, Kansas.

WRESTLING INVENTORY							
No.	Item	Size	Poor	Good	New	Purchased	Total
1							
2							
3							
4							
5							
6							
7							
8							
9							
10							
11							
12							
13							
14							
15							
16							
17							
18							
19							
20							

Fig. 4–1. Wrestling Inventory

Wrestling Mats

Atlas: Atlas Athletic Equipment, St. Louis, Mo. National: National Sports Company, Fond du Lac, Wis. Polvonite: Protection Equipment Co., Rochester, N.Y. Premier: Premier Products, River Vale, N.J. Resilite: Resilite Sports Products, Inc.,

Sunbury, Pa. G. D. Richardson Mfg. Company, Fort Collins, Colo.

Practice and Meet Uniforms

Champion Knitwear Company. Championship Wrestling Products. Cliff Keen Wrestling Products. Rawlings Sporting Goods. Roderick, Inc.

Wrestling Shoes

Championship Wrestling Products. Converse Rubber Company, Malden, Mass. Polvonite Wrestling Shoe. Roderick, Inc.

Wrestling Kneeguards

Most of the general sources. Defenders: Defender Company, Philadelphia, Pa. Flarico: John B. Flaherty Co., Inc. Bronx, N.Y.

Wrestling Headguards

Cliff Keen Wrestling Products. Roderick, Inc. Wolverine: R. V. Roberts Company, Colorado Springs, Colo.

Nylon-Coated Practice Uniforms

Championship Wrestling Products. Cliff Keen Wrestling Products. Converse Rubber Company. Roderick, Inc.

Wrestling Clocks

Championship Wrestling Products. Eastman Kodak Company, Rochester, N.Y. Fairplay Scoreboards, Des Moines, Ia. Micmar Co., Libertyville, Ill. Mohawk Timer: Mohawk Valley Sports, Inc., Little Falls, N.Y.

Wrestling Scorebooks

Mohawk Scorebook. NCAA Wrestling Scorebook. Nordskog's: Iowa Sports Supply Co., Cedar Falls, Ia. Roderick, Inc. Zimmerman Scorebook: James L. Zimmerman, West Mifflin, Pa.

Liquid Nutrition

Hustle: Dr. Pepper Company/Hustle Division, Dallas, Tex. Nutrament: Edward Dalton Company, Evansville, Ind. Top Star: Top Star, Inc., Arlington, Tex.

Equipment Issue

Each wrestler must feel a responsibility for the equipment he is issued. Equipment loss is a problem that confronts every coach. The best way to control this problem is to develop pride

WRESTLING EQUIPMENT ISSUE				
NAME _____ PHONE_____				
ADDRESS _____				
Item	Size	Number	Date Issued	Date Checked In

Fig. 4–2. Individual Wrestling Equipment Issue

in the appearance of the team and constantly stress that issued equipment is for the team to use, not for individuals to misuse.

The second step in controlling equipment loss is to have an efficient system for the issuing and checking in of equipment. Carelessness in this procedure is a primary reason for equipment loss at many schools. Keep a written record of every item that is issued. After the initial issue provide clean equipment only when a soiled item is turned in for cleaning.

File the individual wrestling equipment issue forms alphabetically in a loose-leaf binder. They are then available for speedy reference and can be easily removed when equipment is turned in.

When wrestling items are purchased, they should be marked before being issued for control, and for help in planning future purchases. A suggested procedure is to mark each equipment item with the school name, initial, or nickname; the year of purchase; and a number from within a sequence covering the number of items purchased of a given kind.

Purchasing the practice uniforms in different colors is helpful in issuing equipment. Each size is obtained in a different color. The sizes can be readily sorted and issued to the wrestlers without time wasted looking for the size tags which are frequently lost after a few washings.

Care of Equipment

The very nature of wrestling makes cleanliness a necessity. Wrestling uniforms, practice and meet, should be washed after every use. Headgears, knee pads, and shoes should also be washed frequently. Proper care of equipment will enhance the personal hygiene of the participants as well as increase the life of the equipment. Mats must be cleaned daily. A solution of mild soap and water has proven to be very effective. Serious skin infections may occur if proper maintenance of equipment and facilities is not observed.

All equipment should be kept in the best possible repair. Repair at the first sign of breakage or tearing will prolong the life of equipment.

Directions should always be carefully followed when washing wrestling items. When purchasing new equipment, request written washing instructions and provide this information to the person or company that does the cleaning.

Proper storage and handling of wrestling equipment is essential. Company directions should be explicitly followed. Most mat companies recommend that the wrestling mat be laid flat when not in use. Instructions from the mat companies relative to rolling and unrolling mats must be adhered to for the life of the mat to be prolonged.

A dry rather than moist area is recommended for storing wrestling equipment. Shelves and compartments for the various pieces of equipment help immeasurably in properly storing equipment both in and out of season. Proper security in the equipment storage area should be maintained at all times. Storage shelves, bins, and compartments are best secured with padlocks. The combinations or keys for these padlocks should be available only to the coach and person(s) responsible for the school's equipment issue.

5

Teaching and Coaching Tips

INTRODUCTION

Wrestling's special appeal is its individual challenge and sense of personal achievement, which can be enjoyed equally by the participant or the spectator. It also is an exciting team sport since the result of each wrestler's match determines the team's score. This dual feature has helped increase wrestling's popularity.

Spectator enthusiasm for wrestling has grown as people have become familiar with the techniques and as they have learned the team scoring procedures.

Wrestling is a safe combative sport. It is a contact sport, but it is regulated by rules which prohibit physical punishment. Contestants are not permitted to use holds or maneuvers which would cause an injury.

The ultimate objective in wrestling is to gain a fall. This factor contributes to the excitement of the sport. Regardless of how far behind a wrestler is in his match, he can win at any time by holding his opponent's shoulders to the mat for the required length of time. This suspense heightens the excitement for the fans. It is truly a sport which is never over until the match is completed. Although scores during a match between two skilled opponents are frequently low, scoring rules are such that a scoring maneuver can develop from any position on the mat within a few seconds.

Wrestling can be enjoyed by those with limited abilities as well as by the skilled performer. A beginner can quickly learn the basic techniques. The skilled performer is challenged by the complexity of wrestling maneuvers.

Wrestlers execute moves from the three basic wrestling positions: neutral, offensive, and defensive. Each contestant should become proficient in executing moves which will put his opponent on the mat from a neutral position. A wrestler must also be able to wrestle from the two referee's positions. In the disadvantage or bottom position, he must be able to get away from his opponent or carry out a move which will put him in the advantage position. A wrestler who is in the advantage or top position must know how to keep control of his opponent and, at the same time, attempt pinning combinations which will lead to either a fall or near fall and predicament points. In addition to the offensive moves, each wrestler must know counters and blocks which will counteract the maneuvers of his opponent.

A skilled wrestler must be able to apply a variety of offensive and defensive holds from each wrestling position during the course of a match. His effectiveness will be determined by more than just the number of moves he knows and can apply. He must develop continuity in his moves and integrate his maneuvers into the pattern which occurs in the course of a match. The trademark of a good wrestler is his ability to capitalize on an opponent's mistakes and take immediate advantage of any opening which presents itself. Only through experience and many hours of practice on wrestling moves and counters can a wrestler become skilled in turning an opponent's offensive move to his own advantage. Wrestlers will find that they will be more proficient with some moves than with others. This is to be expected due to physical characteristics and personal likes and dislikes. Every wrestler should be exposed to a variety of moves. This gives him an opportunity to find the ones which he can use with best success and helps him defend against any move he meets in the course of a match.

There are certain basic attributes, other than skilled performance, which characterize a good wrestler. Naturally, each attribute will vary from weight class to weight class and from individual to individual. One advantage wrestling has is that it is possible for a boy who is weak in one area to be successful by concentrating on developing another area. Physical attributes such as balance, coordination, quickness and strength are important. Ability to apply the proper leverage at the appropriate time is another attribute of a good wrestler. Physical condition is also of prime importance for success. The so-called intangible personality characteristics such as desire, willingness to put forth maximum effort, and the ability to execute wrestling techniques properly during the heat of competition are other attributes of the good wrestler.

There are many things a wrestler must do to improve. He must spend many hours practicing and drilling on the wrestling skills involved in take-downs, escapes, break-downs and rides, pinning combinations and reversals. Competitive experience against good competition is essential for improvement. A wrestler must also build his body physically by proper use of weight-training techniques and a general conditioning program. It is an axiom of wrestling that a wrestler can improve only as much as his physical condition will permit. Warm-up and conditioning exercise should be included in every wrestler's work-out schedule.

WRESTLING TIPS

There are three separate and distinct areas of wrestling: wrestling in the neutral position, wrestling in the offensive position, and wrestling in the defensive position. The novice and the expert must learn to perform well in each of these areas. Moreover, the present rule structure divides the match into these three areas.

The Neutral Position

It has been shown that the wrestler who earns the first take-down usually wins the match. In addition to the two-point deficit, it is logical that the psychological impact of losing the first take-down could tip the match.

The on-the-feet technique most used today is the single-leg pick-up. The wrestler needs to develop a sound single-leg take-down and several variations of this maneuver as well. However, if the single-leg technique does not fit the wrestler's style, another take-down must be developed as his primary maneuver. Once thought to be the basic take-down, the double-leg tackle is still a sound offensive weapon. It is easily learned. Also, when thrown and countered, it has innumerable variations that can still be executed with a great deal of success. Most important, the take-down used should be proven out in the practice room before it is tried in a match. A smart wrestler should have alternate take-downs in his bag of tricks in case the favorite loses its effectiveness.

Although many authors do not endorse counter wrestling as a primary offensive weapon, its use on the feet has very definite advantages. Many take-downs have been the result of an excellent counter maneuver.

Another phase in the neutral position is knee wrestling. Very often the opponent forces a wrestler to a situation where both are on their knees facing each other, a position set up by a standing take-down attempt that has been countered. The head snapdown is probably the most used technique. Others that have been used with success are the side drag-by and the under-arm variation techniques. Lateral motion is of paramount importance. Few of the above techniques are successful at all if the wrestler attacks straight on; it is imperative for the initiator to move laterally or force his opponent to do so.

In the main, the neutral position demands that the wrestler spend a great deal of time perfecting his maneuvers, that he understands that a sound offense is the best defense.

The Offensive Position

This particular phase has undergone tremendous change in recent years. The stress for the fall has been paramount in the minds of most wrestling people. International competition has made an indelible mark in this respect. As a result, it has also influenced the American style of wrestling and has encouraged greater use of legs when trying for the fall.

The single most important factor to success in the offensive position is "constant harassment." Keeping the bottom man off balance by destroying his base and harassing him at every moment will almost always insure success. The top wrestler must be persistent in breaking the bottom man down and seeking openings for fall situations. Therefore, the types of break-down must relate to the style of pinning combinations used. The bar-arm breakdown variations immediately set up situations for a possible fall situation such as the bar-arm and under-hook stack.

Counter wrestling is not essential for success if the offensive wrestler is clearly superior. However, logic dictates that the bottom wrestler will make numerous fine moves and these will have to be countered, but for the offensive wrestler to rely on counter wrestling in this position very seldom succeeds. It should be mentioned that a great deal of stress should be placed on learning and exercising countering moves during the practice sessions, so that they can be applied quickly and successfully in an actual match.

The wrestler rides his opponent for one ultimate reason, to secure the fall. The public likes to see a fall and thus recent rule changes have been bent toward attempting more and more falls. This trend is beneficial to the development of the American style of wrestling. The wrestler needs to be offensive in every possible way. The riding position enables him to demonstrate this attitude very effectively. One of the basic maneuvers in the riding position is the use of "cutting" or grapevining the near leg with the top wrestler's near leg. This technique enables the top wrestler to control with considerably more ease the moves of the bottom wrestler. The top man should be aware of scoring points by riding time, predicaments and near falls. It takes a great deal of skill, balance, foresight, and strength to ride well.

The Defensive Position

There are apparent disadvantages facing the wrestler in the defensive position. He may be pinned, he may have predicament and near fall points scored against him, or the top man may be awarded riding time points. He may have to take physical and psychological punishment, and he has to carry his own weight and, for the most part, the weight of his opponent. The wrestler must spend considerable energy to free himself from this position. He must develop sound techniques enabling him to obtain the neutral or offensive position.

Stand-up techniques have become more and more emphasized in recent years. This trend has led many wrestling teachers to develop a variety of methods to strengthen stand-up skills while they also develop ways to counter these techniques. One of the most important factors in escaping successfully through the use of the stand-up is the skill of controlling the opponent's hands. Creating a gap between the two wrestlers also should be mentioned in conjunction with this stand-up situation. Whether the defensive man uses the outside or inside leg stand-up, the secret of success lies in controlling the hands of the offensive wrestler.

The second most used technique in escaping is the sit-out and turns. The defensive wrestler, depending upon the situation, has one of two options: he may sit out and turn in or he may sit out and turn out. These maneuvers must be executed with speed. In essence, the participant must learn to cultivate a good escape whether it is a stand-up or a sit-out technique.

Even though reversals are not usually used as often as the escapes by many of the top-notch wrestling coaches, they must not be overlooked. Reversals are a very important part of the repertoire of a good wrestler. He must learn to control his opponent's body even though he is in the defensive position, because, in essence, this is the story of achieving the reversal successfully. The defensive wrestler must learn to use the weight and momentum of the top man for his own use in the execution of the side-roll; he must learn to use the forces of leverage in the execution of the side-switch, and he must learn to use the opponents' hips as points of reference in the execution of the hip-out maneuvers. All of these must be practiced as often as possible.

Again, the time spent in countering the defensive techniques within the escape and reversal phases is almost as important as the offensive use.

CONCLUSION

The above has been discussed in an effort to familiarize the teacher or coach with basic thoughts about each of the three areas of wrestling in respect to the six phases: pinning combinations, reversals, breakdowns and rides, escapes, knee takedowns, and standing takedowns. The main idea is that the wrestler, to be successful, must attempt to be offensive in all three areas of stress. He must attempt to get that first takedown; he must work vigorously for a fall with a safe and solid ride; and he must not stay in the defensive position on the mat. If the participant adds to this offensive thought the defensive considerations of countering in all the phases, he will have accepted the philosophy that wrestling is one hundred per cent alertness together with constant awareness of where you are and where you feel your opponent will be.

6

Teaching and Coaching Methods

The successful wrestling program is characterized by coaching and teaching methods which are varied to challenge the wrestler, and stimulate and maintain interest. Carefully planned and applied methods also make the best use of time, space, and facilities. Listed below are various methods which will help the instructor plan class periods and practice sessions.

CONDITIONING AND WARM-UP PROCEDURES

Time should be spent on warm-up and conditioning in every practice and class session. While wrestling itself contributes to physical fitness, which is essential to a successful wrestler, a planned program of body conditioning provides sustained fitness and endurance.

It is recommended that a brief warm-up period of light calisthenics, and individual and dual drills begin the practice session, and that conditioning calisthenics end the practice session. All areas of the body should receive attention when giving calisthenics. However, a hard session of calisthenics prior to drilling will detract from the benefit the wrestler receives from the teaching session.

Stretching Exercises—Figs. 6–1 to 6–4

Stretching exercises should precede sustained endurance exercises used in the warm-up drills. There are several techniques

Fig. 6–1.   Sitting Hamstring Stretch

a. Place hands behind the head.

b. Spread legs as wide as possible.

c. Force head toward mat in a bobbing manner.

Attempt to keep knees locked. Individual may touch both elbows to knees or elbows to opposite knees. Place elbow on the mat outside of opposite knee to increase the amount of twisting.

Fig. 6–2.   Hurdler Stretch

a. Extend one leg forward.

b. Place other leg backward, putting the heel under the buttocks.

c. Bend forcefully toward the extended leg.

Repeat exercise with other leg forward.

Fig. 6–3. Upright Hamstring Stretch

a. **Spread legs.**

b. **Bend forward placing stress on the hamstrings.**

To incorporate trunk twisting, the individual should rotate his upper body with maximum stress in all directions.

Fig. 6–4. Straddle Stretch

a. **Extend one leg forward and the other to the rear.**

b. **Place weight of upper body over forward leg.**

c. **Force buttocks toward the mat in order to stretch the muscles in the groin area.**

that can be administered to ensure greater flexibility in the wrestler. Trunk twisting, arm rotating, and leg spreading are a few of the popular methods. The pictures in this section give the reader some of the basic stretching exercises.

Buddy Conditioning Drills—Figs. 6–5 to 6–9

Traditional wrestling exercises like the neck bridges, and straight back lifts should be emphasized to strengthen parts of the body that many students have failed to properly develop.

Conditioning drills should incorporate wrestling techniques whenever possible because they serve the dual function of improving skills and physical condition. There are a number of drills which accomplish this objective.

Spinning Drill—Figs. 6–10 and 6–11

One wrestler assumes the referee's down position. The top wrestler places his chest on the back of the down wrestler and rotates quarter or half turns on the instructor's command. Another method is to have the defensive wrestler lie on his stomach and have the top wrestler spin in the same fashion. This drill helps develop agility and balance for the top wrestler.

Floating Drill

The starting position of the wrestlers will be the same as for the spin drill. The bottom wrestler crawls forward, does partial sitouts, and turns in a circular manner. The top wrestler moves with him and attempts to keep his chest in contact with the bottom wrestler in a balanced position. It is suggested that the wrestlers begin by going ten seconds at a time and then increase the number of repetitions and length of each repetition as their condition and skill improve.

Handfighting Drill

This drill can be executed in the neutral position on the feet, in the neutral position on the knees, or in the referee's position. On a timed basis, two wrestlers in the neutral position attempt to tie up the wrists of the opposing wrestler. This is an excellent drill for strengthening wrists and fingers as well as learning techniques that will assist them.

The same basic drill is executed from the referee's position. The top wrestler initiates break-down maneuvers and the bottom wrestler goes through the counter moves.

Weight-Lifting

Weight-lifting is an important factor in the wrestling conditioning program. It can be used effectively with a large group and in limited facilities. Organize the group so that some members lift weights while other members work on another phase of the class or practice.

Six basic lifts are recommended for wrestlers. Most coaches will probably add others if they have sufficient time and facilities. Suggested lifts to use:

1. Arm Curls.
2. Upright Rowing.
3. Military Press.
4. Bench Press.
5. Partial Squats; place a bench or chair under the buttocks, so the legs of the wrestler will not form an angle less than 90°.
6. Weighted sit-ups.

The amount of weight a boy uses for each lift will be determined initially by his beginning strength. To increase strength the overload principle of physiology must be applied. A general rule to follow is to have the wrestlers start doing three sets of eight repetitions at each lift. When they can do three sets of twelve repetitions on that lift, the weight is increased five or ten pounds and a similar procedure followed. From an organizational standpoint it is best to assign the wrestlers to a weight lifting station by weight class. Thus, all boys in a weight class lift the same amount of weight, which saves time in changing the weights on the bar. The amount of weight will have to be changed for some of the lifts but not from individual to individual. If a boy is exceptionally strong he can be placed with a higher weight class. An important principle of weight lifting

Fig. 6–5. Back Neck Bridge

a. Bottom wrestler assumes back bridge position.

b. Top wrestler lies across chest or stomach of bottom wrestler.

c. Bottom wrestler raises and lowers back.

As bottom man becomes stronger, top wrestler increases the amount of pressure.

Fig. 6–6. Front Neck Bridge

a. Bottom wrestler assumes front bridge position.

b. Top wrestler lies across the back of bottom man.

c. Bottom wrestler rocks back and forth by pushing with his toes.

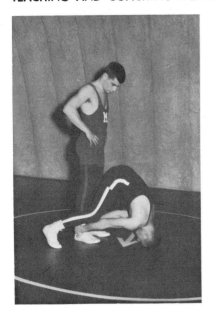

Fig. 6–7. Wrestler's Kip Bridge

a. Wrestler assumes front-bridge position, grasps the ankles of his buddy, and throws legs to end in a back neck bridge.

b. From the back-bridge position the wrestler snaps his legs toward his buddy by forcibly contracting his stomach muscles and at the same time pulling vigorously with his arms, finishing again in the front bridge.

Fig. 6–8. Back Extension Drill

a. Buddy locks legs around wrestler's waist and hands around his neck.

b. Wrestler bends forward and then powerfully extends his back to the starting position.

Fig. 6–9. Power Leg Lift Drill

a. Wrestler grabs his buddy behind the knees and under the thighs. At the same time he lowers his center of gravity.

b. He lifts his buddy to an upright position by powerfully extending his legs.

Fig. 6–10. Spinning Drill — a

Fig. 6–11. Spinning Drill — b

is to give the body sufficient rest. Wrestlers should lift only on alternate days.

Isometrics

Opinions vary on the value of isometrics for wrestlers. A common criticism is that the muscles do not work through their entire range of movement. This prevents total muscle development and does not contribute as much as isotonic exercise with regard to increasing and maintaining body strength. Some physiologists have questioned the advisability of using isometrics because of the excessive strain placed on tendons and ligaments.

An advantage of isometric exercise is that strength is developed rapidly with a minimum of exercise time. Another advantage is that team isometrics do not require equipment and can be given in limited quarters and by an assistant. It is suggested that the exercises be started at six seconds in duration and increased to twelve seconds. There should be exercises for each of the major muscle groups with special emphasis on such areas as the neck and upper arms, where wrestlers have greater need for strength. There is no doubt that strength can be increased dramatically through proper use of isometric exercise. The exercises should be comparable to the lifts that are recommended for wrestlers when weight lifting.

Use of combined isometric–isotonic exercise is gaining acceptance. The procedure is to initiate the muscular action with an isometric contraction and then conclude it isotonically. Mechanical devices for this type of exercise are being sold; however, manual techniques are possible if a machine is not available. Have the wrestler do an isometric contraction with one of the lifts. Upon completion of the contraction, he should immediately move to a weight lifting bar and do one set of this lift isotonically.

Apparatus

A resourceful wrestling coach will utilize pieces of gymnastic equipment in his conditioning program. The rope, parallel bars, high bar, and side horse are examples of gymnastic pieces that wrestlers can use. Specific exercises or routines should be required on each piece. As an example, each boy might be required to climb the rope a specified number of times, do dips on the parallel bar, pull-ups on the high bar, and leg circles on the side horse.

Running—Figs. 6–12 and 6–13

Running is basic to a wrestling conditioning program. If your school has no indoor track, use corridors, bleachers or stairs. They are ideal for this purpose. Running is another activity which the coach or teacher with overcrowded facilities can use to good advantage by splitting the class or squad.

Running in place can be used if the running area outside the wrestling room is inadequate. A good technique to use is to run on a timed basis. It is suggested that the wrestlers accelerate to top speed for ten seconds and then slow to a jog for ten seconds and repeat as many times as physical condition will permit.

Rope Skipping

Rope skipping is an excellent conditioner for wrestling. By varying the type of jumps, this activity can be an interesting challenge to the wrestlers as well as an excellent technique for developing coordination and cardio-vascular endurance.

Individual Spinning Drill—Fig. 6–14

The wrestler assumes a position on his side with his arms tucked in and his knees brought up toward his chest. On the leader's command, the wrestler spins rapidly in a tight circle and on a subsequent command, he rolls to his opposite side and continues spinning. This is an excellent technique for developing the wrestler's ability to "move out" on side sit-out situations in a competitive experience.

Man-on-Shoulders Drill—Fig. 6–15

Pair the wrestlers according to weight. Place one wrestler on the other wrestler's shoulders, stressing that the individual doing the lifting keeps a "straight back" and lifts with his legs. The

Fig. 6—12.   Running in Place — a

Fig. 6—13.   Running in Place — b

Fig. 6–14.   Individual Spinning Drill

Fig. 6–15.   Man-on-Shoulders
Drill

purpose of the drill is two-fold: to strengthen the thigh muscles of the leg by doing *partial* bends at the knee, and to strengthen the calf muscles of the lower leg by doing heel raises.

SITUATIONAL DRILLS

Most practice sessions should include a period of time devoted to situational drills. The number of drills and the time spent can vary from situation to situation. Drilling is essential if the wrestlers are to develop a variety of moves for use in competition. When coaches fail to spend sufficient time on this phase of their program, the skill development of their wrestlers is retarded. The challenge is to make the drills as interesting and varied as possible. Boredom can negate the benefits which normally accompany drills on wrestling techniques.

Initial Maneuver Drills

When a new move is being taught, first demonstrate the proper execution. Next, break down the move into its component parts. For beginning groups it is advisable to practice the move initially by using the number system. On the first number, all members of the group execute the first part of the move. This is followed by the second part of the move and so on until the entire move is completed. This technique makes it possible for the coach or teacher to check each member of the class or team on all phases of that move. Although many wrestling maneuvers can be executed in different ways, every wrestling move demands that certain basic principles be followed. By utilizing the above technique it is possible to assist the wrestler in learning the proper execution of the move and improving his chance for success when he applies the maneuver in competition. During this learning phase the wrestler's opponent should give only enough resistance to make the move realistic.

Counter Drills

Good wrestling is predicated on the wrestler's being offensive-minded. It is suggested that the scoring move be practiced and learned thoroughly before the counters are given. If the counters are given too soon, it will discourage many wrestlers from trying different moves. Once counters are given they should be taught in the same manner as the offensive moves. Break them down into their component parts against passive resistance and then gradually test them against increasing resistance.

A good counter drill to use is to call out the initial move and have the defensive wrestler throw the counter when his opponent initiates the designated move. The wrestler executing the first move should gradually increase his speed as the competency of the counter wrestler improves.

Another good drill to use when practicing counters is to set up a series of counter moves that are commonly experienced in competition. An example would be a roll–reroll–switch–reswitch grouping. These moves are practiced in the following order. First, the roll is executed; secondly, the roll–reroll; next, the roll–reroll–switch; and fourth, the roll–reroll–switch–reswitch is executed in its entirety.

Continuity Drill

This type of drill is designed to instill the idea that a good wrestler must be able to move immediately from one move to another. Seldom will the first move work in good wrestling competition. It is imperative that the wrestler looks for the next opening when his initial move is stopped. As an example, a long sit-out will frequently leave the top wrestler out of position and perhaps set up for a far-side roll. Each coach can develop his own grouping of moves to develop this proficiency. Emphasize that if the first move doesn't work go immediately to the next one. The following are moves which can be used for this type of drill.

1. Inside stand up–tear hands–switch–step behind.
2. Far side roll–switch–step back.
3. Short sit out–turn in–front sit out–granby roll.

The opponent of the wrestler making the moves should be instructed to block the first moves, allowing the final one to be completed.

Single-Leg Reaction Drill—Figs. 6–16 to 6–18

The wrestlers assume a standing takedown position. A towel, headguard, or kneepad is placed near one of the defensive wrestler's legs. The offensive wrestler attempts to penetrate straight in on a single-leg sweep maneuver. The objective is for him to reach in behind the leg and grab the towel before the defensive wrestler picks it up.

Blindfold Drill

Place a blindfold over one of the wrestlers and have him execute any of the above drills. This is excellent for developing balance, kinesthetic feel, and movement anticipation.

FULL-GO WRESTLING

Boys participate in wrestling because they like the challenge of using their physical abilities and wrestling techniques to get the best of their opponent. Although drills and conditioning are essential, the boys will learn to wrestle and achieve maximum improvement only when they have the opportunity to get on the mat and oppose someone in a wrestling match. There are nu-

Fig. 6–16. Single-Leg Reaction Drill — a

Fig. 6–17.   Single-Leg Reaction Drill — b

Fig. 6–18.   Single-Leg Reaction Drill — c

merous special methods that can be used for improvement and assist the boys in becoming skilled wrestlers.

It is best to have boys wrestle one weight class below and one class above their actual weight. Any greater weight difference can prove dangerous to the smaller wrestler. There are exceptions, but this principle should be followed in most cases. Wrestlers should learn to wrestle against smaller, quicker opponents as well as larger, stronger individuals. This combination tends to develop a wrestler's skills more rapidly. Wrestling less skilled opponents so new moves can be used, and wrestling better wrestlers to challenge his ability aids the wrestler's over-all development.

Ladder Wrestling

Pair off eight or ten wrestlers in either the neutral or referee's position. One member of each pair will remain in the same area at the end of the timed period and his opponent will move up to the next person. This drill will continue until each moving wrestler has wrestled all stationary wrestlers. The length of each period can be varied to fit the drill into the practice plan.

Spurt Wrestling

In this drill the coach or teacher limits the length of the period to 10 or 15 seconds. Wrestlers concentrate on wrestling all-out for this short period. This is a good drill to use when simulating meet conditions.

Spurt wrestling also can be used as a competition drill. Award a point for an escape or reversal and a point for riding out the period. Designate a defensive group to challenge an offensive group.

Two-Take-Down Drill

By having two boys wrestle until one wrestler gets two takedowns, it is often possible to obtain maximum effort from the wrestlers. It might be necessary to have a time limit when the boys are evenly matched.

Champion Drill

One wrestler is challenged by 3 or 4 others. The wrestler who is challenged starts from the same position against each opponent. This drill can be used effectively when one boy is far superior to the rest of the boys near his weight class. This technique will give him a good work-out.

Quick Escapes

In this drill, the down wrestler attempts to gain an escape within a short, designated time limit. A fast, hard initial effort is the objective.

Quick Escapes with Penalties

This drill is the same as the above except that the offensive wrestler receives a penalty such as requiring him to execute 6 long sit-outs if he fails to control the defensive wrestler and the defensive wrestler receives the same penalty if he fails to escape.

Round-Robin Take-Downs

One wrestler stays on the mat until he is taken down. Three or four different wrestlers are given a chance to take him down before a new "king" is placed on the mat. When a challenging wrestler gets a take-down he becomes the king. It is best to set a limit to the number of take-downs the king is allowed.

Odd-Man Rotation Drill

Wrestlers are arranged in groups of three. One wrestler is in the defensive wrestler's position and another is in the offensive position. After one minute of wrestling the offensive wrestler becomes the defensive wrestler and the defensive wrestler moves off the mat and a fresh wrestler comes in to the offensive position. This rotation continues until the wrestlers have wrestled a desired number of minutes. The position of the wrestlers can be alternated so they do not wrestle opponents in the same position each time they are on the mat.

Look-Away Drill

This drill is very effective in forcing wrestlers to try different moves. Many times a wrestler will depend on one or two moves and fail to develop other moves. The coach or instructor signals wrestler B to look away and then through use of hand signals indicates to wrestler A what his first move will be. Both wrestlers will wrestle all-out when the whistle blows. Ten seconds are sufficient for each attempt.

Matches

It is important throughout the season to wrestle some full-length and some over-length matches. The use of short periods totalling a regulation match or more can be highly beneficial. This is particularly true when the squad is large and time and space are limited. Competitors can go much harder during the short periods and will usually wrestle more aggressively. This is actually an application of the track interval-training technique.

FREE-TIME WRESTLING

All wrestlers enjoy "rolling around" on the mat. Make provisions for this type of wrestling. The wrestlers have an opportunity to practice the moves and can help each other considerably. This type of wrestling also has many psychological benefits for the participants. They can wrestle in a relaxed manner and smooth out their problems in an ideal learning situation. A practical application of this method is its use the day preceding or the day following a match.

Chain Wrestling on the Mat

This term refers to wrestling which is continuous in nature and is carried out in a non-competitive manner. Both wrestlers practice their moves and strive to develop skill in keeping a continuous "chain" of moves going. This might be called a laboratory for practical application of the moves and counters learned in situational drills. It is advisable to have experienced wrestlers chain wrestle with inexperienced wrestlers. This procedure helps considerably in the development of the inexperienced wrestler.

Dummy Wrestling from the Neutral Position

This is similar to chain wrestling on the mat with the exception that after a take-down and the following counter, the wrestlers move back to the neutral position. Special emphasis is placed on setting up the take-down properly and following through into a pinning combination or good ride. Emphasis can also be placed on what is termed the four-point or five-point take-down; they are take-down with a predicament, and take-down with a near-fall.

Part II

THEORY OF
TEACHING
WRESTLING

7

Organizing, Administering, and Evaluating

GENERAL OBJECTIVES OF A WRESTLING PROGRAM

Proper execution of beginning wrestling techniques.

Development of a desirable level of physical fitness.

Development of an interest in amateur wrestling.

Development of an understanding and appreciation for amateur wrestling.

Ability to wrestle competitively in an acceptable manner.

QUALITIES OF A WRESTLING TEACHER

Knowledge of wrestling techniques.

Ability to adequately demonstrate basic maneuvers.

Ability to organize and use unit of instruction and daily lesson plans.

Knowledge and understanding of needs, desires, interests, and maturation levels of his students.

Good personal health.

Adequate voice.

Ability to establish rapport with class and present information in a meaningful way.

Sincere belief in the values of wrestling.

Proper perspective of the total educational program of the school.

CLASS PROCEDURES

Most of the procedures used in a wrestling class will be similar to procedures used in other physical education classes. The nature of wrestling, however, requires special provisions in some areas. Proper teaching progression of wrestling must take place to minimize the chance of injury which can occur if students attempt to wrestle before they acquire proper skills. A teacher of wrestling must also carefully pair off participants so they are of comparable ability and size. This is important from the safety standpoint. Class morale will be increased when this procedure is followed.

Roll Call

Squad or spot methods are recommended for speed in taking attendance. Calling student names initially will help the instructor to quickly know the members of the class. Regardless of the technique used an instructor should spend no more than one or two minutes of the class time taking roll.

Warm-Up

A brief period of time should be devoted to stretching and general warm-up procedures. It is recommended that bridging and high bends be used together with two different exercises each day. (Calisthenics may be administered at the end of the class time.)

Drilling

This portion of the class period should be devoted to teaching the moves to be covered in the course. Chapter 6 contains procedures that can be used when teaching the moves. It is preferable to demonstrate and explain the move first. The demonstration–explanation should be followed immediately by class practice in executing the move. Previously learned moves should be reviewed each period. Review old moves first, then present the new ones. The number of new moves presented will be determined by the speed with which the class is able to master the various skill-levels set forth in the class unit of instruction (see p. 74).

Competition

Every class period should have some actual competition. Perhaps the first day will simply be one boy trying to pin his opponent from a half-nelson pinning combination. The time allotted might total four 15-second periods. As the class progresses, more time can be devoted to competitive wrestling and less time spent on drilling moves.

The best way to group a class for drilling and competition is to have the class members line up by weight with the lightest boy at one end of the line and the heaviest boy at the other. In this manner the class members can be divided in groups of different sizes for drills that require three, four, or five boys.

It is desirable to coordinate the wrestling unit with the intramural wrestling tournament. The tournament should be held near the end of the wrestling unit and class members should be encouraged to participate. If an intramural tournament is not held, have members of different physical education classes compete, using regulation meet conditions perhaps with modifications in the length of the matches. Wrestling a member of another class stimulates interest.

The students must be appropriately attired for wrestling. They should wear the regulation physical education costume with athletic supporter, athletic socks, and high top gym shoes. The instructor should have a firm policy in regard to clean uniforms. This is important from the standpoint of aesthetic values for the class and for personal hygiene.

Class discipline can be achieved and maintained if the students are properly motivated and challenged. The drill portions of the class period should move rapidly and lead up to the competitive situation where the students apply the skills they have learned. This approach assists the teacher immeasurably in making it an interesting class. The teacher should vary the drills and approach to prevent boredom.

CURRICULUM DESIGNS

Junior and senior high school physical education curricula are characteristically composed of a number of activity units geared to the student's maturational level. These activities are taught in a progressive fashion from grade level to grade level. The skills learned at one particular grade level help form the foundation for the more advanced skills in future years. A program set up in this manner will be designed primarily to meet the needs and interests of the students at each of the grade levels.

Physical education course units are designed to meet seasonal needs. In the fall the curriculum might, for example, include units of instruction in soccer and touch football. The next segment most likely would be indoors and traditionally includes stunts and tumbling, volleyball, some form of dancing, and wrestling.

The purpose of this discussion is to emphasize that wrestling must be an integral instructional unit of the over-all curriculum encompassing the seventh to the twelfth grades. Wrestling could begin in the elementary school curriculum on a limited basis. Therefore, it is important for the physical educator to understand that wrestling as well as many other activities has a wealth of material that should be presented to the student in a piecemeal fashion so that proper continuity takes place from one grade level to the next. This avoids repetition and makes it possible to delve deeper in the sport each year. This is the sophisticated approach to the teaching of wrestling. The units do not need to exceed five weeks in length, and may be as few as three weeks in the junior high program if classes meet every day.

The following is a program outlining general areas for each of the grade levels from seventh to twelfth.

SEVENTH GRADE UNIT ON WRESTLING—3 WEEKS

1. Balance and floating drills.
2. Values of wrestling.
3. Referee's position on the mat.
4. Two basic falls and counters.
5. Two basic reversals and counters.
6. Basic neutral stance.
7. Two basic take-downs and counters.
8. Basic rules and regulations.

EIGHTH GRADE UNIT ON WRESTLING—3 WEEKS

1. Balance and floating drills.
2. Values of wrestling.

3. Referee's position on the mat.
4. Three falls and counters.
5. Three reversals and counters.
6. Two basic escapes and counters.
7. Basic neutral stance.
8. Three take-downs and counters.
9. Basic rules and regulations.

NINTH-GRADE UNIT OF WRESTLING—4 WEEKS

1. History of wrestling.
2. Values of wrestling.
3. Balance drills.
4. Basic neutral and referee's positions.
5. Three falls and counters.
6. Three reversals and counters.
7. Two basic rides.
8. Three escapes and counters.
9. Three take-downs and counters.
10. Basic rules and regulations.

TENTH-GRADE UNIT ON WRESTLING—5 WEEKS

1. Basic rules and regulations.
2. Values of wrestling.
3. History of wrestling.
4. Points about officiating.
5. Basic maneuvers in all phases of wrestling.[1]
6. Counters to all the phases.
7. Varsity program qualifications.

ELEVENTH-GRADE UNIT ON WRESTLING—5 WEEKS

1. Basic rules and regulations.
2. Values of wrestling.
3. History of wrestling.
4. Points about officiating.
5. Basic maneuvers in all phases of wrestling.[1]
6. Counters to all the phases.
7. Description of different styles of wrestling.

TWELFTH-GRADE UNIT ON WRESTLING—5 WEEKS

1. Basic rules and regulations.

2. Values of wrestling.
3. History of wrestling.
4. Officiating and understanding of match workings.
5. Basic maneuvers in all phases of wrestling.[1]
6. Counters to all the phases.
7. Description of different styles of wrestling.

The authors wish to suggest a new approach divorced from the traditional design in presenting the techniques of wrestling. It is recommended that mat wrestling precede wrestling on the feet. This is advisable from the standpoint of safety and also to instill the proper emphasis of wrestling, going for the fall.

UNIT OF INSTRUCTION

Developing a unit of instruction is a major project for any teacher of education. In the area of physical education, and particularly in wrestling, the unit has its uniqueness because the teacher is not only attempting to present the history, values, rules and regulations of the sport, but he must be able to teach how to execute a particular skill with some degree of proficiency.

As a result the physical educator must have a working knowledge of the many facets of wrestling as well as a knowledge of skill performance in the activity. This difficult task hampers many educators in the field. Thus, it is essential to construct a plan of action in all activities in order to properly instruct in the activity. This appproach will aid the inexperienced teacher in presenting the unit.

The unit of instruction in wrestling follows a basic outline agreed upon by the authorities in the field of physical education as being functionally sound. The following is an outline which can be utilized in developing a unit of instruction in physical education.

---

[1] Continued emphasis on stressing the progression from elementary to more difficult techniques.

Outline for a Unit of Instruction

Situation Data

  I. Orientation
    A. Historical development
    B. Values
    C. Teaching aids
    D. Taking stock
  II. Objectives
    A. Teacher objectives
    B. Student objectives
 III. Planning Periods
    A. Work periods
    B. Lesson periods
 IV. Evaluation (see p. 82)
    A. Subjective evaluation
      1. practical examination
      2. integrated performance
    B. Objective evaluation
      1. written examination
      2. tournament competition
    C. Grading Procedures

Sample of Unit of Instruction on Wrestling

Situation Data
    Grade level, 9
    Number of weeks, 4
    Periods per week, 3
    Length of period, 50 minutes
    Equipment, 24 x 24-ft mat with additional side mats
    Number of students, 32

  I. Orientation
    A. Historical development
      1. Wrestling is one of the oldest forms of combat of which we
        we have any record.

2. This sport, in a systematic and scientific form, was probably introduced into Greece from Asia or Egypt.

3. Although wrestling is one of our oldest sports, it did not come into prominence as an amateur sport in the U.S. until recent years.

4. The first organized intercollegiate contest was held between the Universities of Pennsylvania and Yale in 1900.

5. Today wrestling is an international sport and two types are sponsored in the competition: free-style and Greco-Roman.

6. General reference: see Chapter 1 and the bibliography.

B. Values of Wrestling

1. Most boys, regardless of size, can compete in wrestling.

2. Body build does not limit a boy's chances in competing.

3. Wrestling is one of the best sports for developing physical fitness.

4. It is an activity which can aid in the development of one's personality traits.

C. Teaching Aids

1. Discuss and explain nomenclature, rules and maneuvers by means of:

a. films (see bibliography)
b. blackboard
c. picture cards
d. bulletin board

2. The use of competent students or varsity competitors is of benefit for demonstration purposes.

3. Hand-out material will give assistance in explaining the history, values, techniques, and rules and regulations.

D. Taking Stock

1. Determining the amount of knowledge students have acquired by:

a. question-and-answer session
b. general knowledge test on wrestling

2. Have the students display their wrestling abilities to give you an appraisal of their skill.

3. Determine their weight classes by having them weigh in during the first- or second-class session.

II. Objectives

A. Teacher Objectives

1. To meet student needs and interests.
2. To acquaint students with the knowledge and appreciation of wrestling.
3. To make students physically fit to wrestle a brief match without undue fatigue.
4. To teach the basic skills of wrestling

B. Student Objectives
1. To secure some knowledge and appreciation of wrestling.
2. To utilize this activity as a means of becoming physically fit.
3. To receive some enjoyment and fun from the activity.
4. To learn and retain some basic techniques that will aid in self-defense and contribute to self-confidence.

III. Planning Periods
A. Work periods
1. This unit will be four weeks in length, having three classes a week for a total of twelve class hours.
2. The first week will be devoted to orientation, the next two weeks to skill acquisition, and the last week to competition and evaluation.

B. Lesson Plans
Lesson No. 1
1. Written test for taking stock.
2. Film on basic techniques—15 minutes.
3. Brief history on wrestling hand-out.
4. Weigh the class on scales.
5. Discussion and demonstration of illegal holds.
Lesson No. 2
1. Review last class period by question–answer session.
2. Values of wrestling.
3. Referee's position, offensive and defensive positions.
4. Balance and floating drills.
5. Demonstration of side-switch.
Lesson No. 3
1. Review last class period, referee's position and side-switch.
2. Demonstration and execution of side-roll and sit-out to crawfish.
3. Counters to the reversals.
4. Calisthenics.

Lesson No. 4

1. Review reversals and counters.
2. Demonstration and execution of near-side ride and two-on-one ride.
3. Counters to the rides.
4. Reversal drills.

Lesson No. 5

1. Review rides and counters.
2. Demonstration of sit-outs for escapes.
3. Execution of the escapes.
4. Counters to the escapes.

Lesson No. 6

1. Review of escapes and counters.
2. Demonstration of the stand-up techniques.
3. Execution of the stand-up.
4. Counter to the stand-up.
5. Escape drills.

Lesson No. 7

1. Review of stand-up and counters.
2. Demonstration of half-nelson and crotch; bar-arm and under-hook; and reverse cradle.
3. Execution of the falls.
4. One minute matches.

Lesson No. 8

1. Review of the falls.
2. Discussion of the counters to the falls.
3. Execution of the fall counters.
4. Demonstration of the basic neutral stance.
5. Drill for touching the knees for take-down set-ups.

Lesson No. 9

1. Review of take-down set-up.
2. Demonstration and execution of double-leg drop; single-leg drop; and duck-under.
3. Counters to the take-downs.
4. Round-robin take-downs.

Lesson No. 10

1. Drills for warming up.

2. First and second round matches in the class tournament.[2]

Lesson No. 11

1. Drills for warming up.
2. Final round of matches for the class tournament.[2]
3. It is best to go just three 1-minute periods with two matches going on at the same time.

Lesson No. 12

1. Written examination—15 minutes.
2. Practical examination—35 minutes.

IV. Evaluation
  A. Subjective evaluation
    1. Practical examination (skill test)—20 points.
    2. Integrated performance noted during the tournament rounds —35 points.
  B. Objective evaluation
    1. Written examination—25 points.
    2. Number of wins in the tournament—20 points.
    Total A and B—100 points.
  C. Grading Procedures
    A 92–100 points.
    B 85–91 points.
    C 77–84 points.
    D 70-76 points.
    F below 70 points.

WRESTLING IN THE INTRAMURAL PROGRAM

Wrestling is ideal for a high school intramural program. A tournament held at the end of the wrestling unit in physical education classes heightens interest in the sport and gives students a goal and a lively opportunity to apply the techniques learned in class.

A tournament can be held for each grade level. This approach, together with adhering to the weight classifications, will equalize competition and allow for greater participation.

---

[2] With a class of thirty-two students, it is quite probable that weight divisions set up by grouping similar size boys should not exceed seven.

The methods by which teams are formed should follow the established pattern of other sports. Selection might be the home room, the physical education class, or perhaps on an arbitrarily assigned basis if this is the school intramural policy.

The best intramural wrestling set-up is an open tournament, permitting all interested boys to wrestle regardless of the number in each weight class. On a team basis, there is sometimes a restriction of one entry per weight class. This violates the basic principle of maximum participation in an intramural program.

The purposes of an intramural tournament are varied. The boy who doesn't make the wrestling team still has an athletic outlet, and an opportunity for competition beyond that offered in the class period. Intramurals also provide all interested students with a continued opportunity for wrestling. Because many varsity programs are not large enough to provide a place for every boy who wants to wrestle, intramurals may fill the void.

Intramurals can assist the varsity coach in a variety of ways, and therefore should complement and be closely coordinated with the interscholastic wrestling program as well as the basic instructional program. The late maturing boy, for example, can continue to wrestle and perhaps develop the ability to eventually gain a slot on the school team. Intramural wrestling can also help the high school coach spot promising wrestlers with varsity potential.

Finding time to hold intramural activities is a problem in most high schools. They are scheduled at various times—before school, during the lunch hour, after school, or on Saturdays. It is best to offer supervised intramural wrestling on a non-tournament basis during as many of these times as possible. At the end of the intramural time devoted to wrestling, a tournament should be held; scheduled perhaps after school, in the evening, or on Saturday.

The tournament should be properly organized with qualified officials. The finals should be held in the gymnasium in a setting similar to that used for varsity meets. The intramural director, or even the varsity wrestling coach, should present the awards at the end of each championship match.

The type of tournament will depend on a variety of factors: the number of entries, amount of time available, and number of available mats. It is not always feasible to hold a Bagnall-Wild tournament, because of the amount of wrestling which is required. In this case a single elimination tournament or a single elimination with a consolation bracket type of tournament is recommended. The single elimination tournament is the fastest to run, but careful seeding of contestants is required to help make sure the best wrestlers meet in the semi-finals and finals. Another disadvantage of the single elimination is that half of the wrestlers get to wrestle only once. In the single elimination consolation tournament, all wrestlers who lose in the first round are placed in a consolation tournament. This will ensure two matches for every entry. There will be a winner in the championship portion of the tournament as well as in the consolation portion. This can add interest in the tournament.

Another technique which can be followed is to have participants in each weight class divided according to their ability. This is a wise procedure. It encourages more boys to compete because they know they will be wrestling boys of similar ability. This is a basic reason why varsity wrestlers should not be permitted to compete in an intramural wrestling tournament. Moreover, varsity team members have ample opportunities for wrestling competition. Their intramural competition may discourage other wrestlers.

Varsity team members can help run the intramural tournament as timers and scorers. They can also handle many of the administrative details before, during, and after the tournament. They can also be used effectively as coaches.

Official wrestling rules should be followed in an intramural tournament in most instances. However, it is recommended that the periods be shortened. Three periods of 1 minute each can be used successfully. Some intramural directors prefer periods of 1-2-2, or 1-1½-1½. Boys should not wrestle more than their condition will permit. Matches that are too long destroy interest and enthusiasm. There should be only one weigh-in.

For the safety and welfare of the student, the intramural wrestling program must have qualified adult supervision. It is also important that competition is equalized as much as possible. Ability, experience, and level of maturation must be considered as well as weight and grade level of participants.

If wrestling instruction is not provided in the physical education program, provision should be made to provide instruction and conditioning sessions for all contestants prior to the intramural tournament.

EVALUATION

It is harder to evaluate an individual's progress in wrestling than in most sports. There are no exacting or precise yardsticks like bettered scores or lowered times. Wrestling falls more in the subjective areas of evaluation. However, there are some objective measuring techniques; these will be discussed.

Subjective Evaluation

Subjective evaluation which involves on-the-spot observation and follow-through by a critic will benefit the individual wrestler. The value here is that the wrestler generally receives immediate correction of his errors and is shown the proper method of executing the skill. This is a "piece-work" approach and results in a practical examination of specific skills or techniques. Another approach is the integrated style of evaluation in which the participant is observed carefully in a practice session or in competition. The value here is that the wrestler is evaluated under normal wrestling conditions.

Practical Examination. The practical examination is the most successful evaluation technique because specific weaknesses and strengths can be detected immediately. It also offers an opportunity to document the wrestler's progress and alerts him to his deficiencies and efficiencies as they affect his over-all performances.

Grading charts which list the various skills are essential in documenting and measuring a wrestler's progress. The recorded

PRACTICAL EXAMINATION

NAME _____   DATE _____

Techniques	Rating Scale				Comments
	Excel-lent	Good	Fair	Poor	
Standing Take-down (single-leg pick-up)					
Knee Take-down (head snap-down)					
Escape (inside-leg stand-up)					
Reversal (side-switch)					
Ride (Turkish Bar)					
Breakdown (bar-arm and far-ankle)					
Fall (half-nelson and under-hook)					

Fig. 7–1. Practical Examination Chart

ratings on a chart are useful to the individual in his self-evaluation, and they quickly reveal the next best steps to take in developing a wrestler. Above is a typical chart which can be made and kept by a physical education teacher for his wrestling classes.

Integrated Performances. This form of evaluation is generally used during actual matches in both physical education and varsity situations. Again, the observation is handled by an experienced person whose job is to take stock of apparent weaknesses and list them in a note pad as errors occur. His notes serve as a basis for discussion and later for practices, either in a group or with the individual concerned. It also is helpful if the individual wrestler keeps his own records, both mental and written, for they are his self-evaluation tool. Such records make the evaluation process a continuous one, which is essential if the wrestler is to achieve the optimum of his abilities.

Objective Evaluation

In individual sports like archery, bowling and diving, in which the participant has no direct contact with his opponent, individual scores clearly define and measure the level of performance. Team scores provide a poor indication of individual competency. In activities like tennis, fencing and wrestling, the team won-loss record doesn't necessarily mean that the individual members all have polished skills. Particular members may have played poorly in spite of the final score. Thus, a more concrete measurement for evaluating the individual participant's endeavors is necessary. The three techniques most often used are:

1. The statistical approach of what is and what is not being accomplished by each individual (explained in detail in Chapter 9).
2. The won-lost record of an individual in dual and tournament competition.
3. The self-testing approach using a group of study areas to determine specific or general knowledges about the activity.

Individual Won-Lost Record. Taking note of the individual's specific won-lost record can be of great benefit. In the evaluation phase of a unit of instruction, the teacher of wrestling takes particular care in assessing this criterion. Winning the weight class or a certain number of matches should be one of the important means by which participation is evaluated.

Placing the won-lost percentages on the bulletin board for all the members of the class or wrestling squad is often a self-motivating technique. This will readily give the teacher or coach an immediate form of evaluation and at the same time allow for self-evaluation to take place.

Study Area Approach to Measurement. The following is a list of study area questions that can be administered to the student of a wrestling class in the form of a written examination, a very excellent method of objective evaluation. Very often the coach can test the squad by asking them important questions about the rules and regulations or about certain areas that need to be stressed:

1. List five major differences between interscholastic and inter-collegiate wrestling.
2. Name two types of reversals.
3. Explain the difference between Greco-Roman and catch-as-catch-can styles of wrestling.
4. Designate the different ways to score points in a regular match, giving their respective values.
5. List the proper weights used in the NCAA tournament.
6. Why is it necessary to be in properly trained condition before wrestling competitively?
7. What are the values of proper care and maintenance of equipment?
8. Define the term *amateur wrestling*.
9. From which style of wrestling in England did our present-day form of catch-as-catch-can evolve?
10. Name three types of standing take-downs.
11. Why is the defensive position on the mat the worst position?
12. What is meant by the neutral position?
13. Describe two pinning combinations, two escapes, and two rides.
14. List five illegal holds in amateur wrestling.
15. Explain at least five beneficial objectives of wrestling.
16. List the ways by which a team may score points in tournament competition giving their respective values.
17. Why is wrestling considered one of the fastest growing American sports?
18. List five technical violations in wrestling.
19. Define the term *chain wrestling*.
20. Set up an eight-team tournament bracket.

8

Beginning Techniques

It is difficult to estimate the total number of wrestling holds presently being used in competition. The multiplicity of moves used has caused some wrestlers and coaches to overlook the need for a sound wrestling foundation. This chapter presents the wrestling techniques that each wrestler should master before attempting advanced skills. These techniques also develop skills that are applicable to advanced wrestling. Careful analysis of advanced moves shows that similar skills are utilized when executing advanced holds. The coach who has beginning wrestlers or the teacher of a beginning wrestling class will attain maximum group improvement by first teaching the techniques described in this chapter. Wrestlers who have had this background will progress rapidly when they are exposed to advanced moves.

The moves in each skill area are presented in the order the authors recommend they be taught. This unique feature should prove valuable to the beginning teacher and coach. Counter moves are in the latter part of the chapter. This is in line with the philosophy that counter moves should be taught only after the initial move is being properly executed.

The pictures of each technique are accompanied by a brief written description of the important coaching and teaching points that need to be emphasized. The written description will always be referring to the wrestler executing the move. When there are two or more pictures for one particular maneuver, the first letter under the description refers to the first picture, the second letter refers to the second picture, and so on for the complete maneuver. However, when a maneuver has only one picture, all the letters in the description refer to this picture.

The starting position shown in Figures 8–7 and 8–8 is used in international competition and in some meets and tournaments in the United States. It is very possible that it will eventually become the official starting position for intercollegiate and interscholastic wrestling in the United States. The authors, therefore, recommend that coaches give their wrestlers an opportunity to become familiar with this start.

BASIC STANCES

Fig. 8–1. Drop-Step Stance

a. Front foot points directly toward opponent.

b. Back foot approximately 12–15 inches back of front foot and at a 45-degree angle.

c. Arms slightly extended; thumbs inside for opposition.

d. Head tall; back straight and almost upright.

e. One shoulder slightly turned away from opponent.

Fig. 8–2. Square Stance

a. Feet are parallel to each other and slightly wider than hips.

b. Semi-squat position.

c. Head, arms, and hands same as in drop-step stance.

d. Shoulders square.

Fig. 8–3. Long Tie-Up on Feet

a. Face opponent head to head.

b. Control head by placing right arm around the neck with elbow pointing toward mat.

c. Control opponent's right arm by placing arm to inside or by grabbing his wrist; full lock-up, collar and elbow, is not recommended.

Fig. 8–4. Tie-Up Position on Knees

a. Face opponent in ear-to-ear or head-to-head lock-up.

b. Control head as in long tie-up on the feet.

c. Control opponent's right arm by grabbing wrist.

Lateral motion is essential in this position.

REFEREE'S
POSITION

Fig. 8–5.   Offensive Wrestler's Position

a. Right arm around the waist and perpendicular to long axis of defensive wrestler's back, with right hand on his navel.

b. Left hand on and behind the near elbow.

c. Head to the center of defensive wrestler's back.

d. Knees outside invisible plane made by the defensive wrestler's left hand and knee, without touching.

Fig. 8–6.   Defensive Wrestler's Position

a. Hands flat on the mat and at least 12 inches in front of the knees.

b. Knees at approximately shoulder width.

c. Toes in line with the hands and knees, must not be turned in or out of the invisible plane made by the hands and knees.

Fig. 8–7. Offensive Wrestler's Position

a. Hands on the defensive wrestler's back with thumbs touching.

b. He may be:
   1. On both feet.
   2. On both knees.
   3. On one knee and one foot.

Fig. 8–8. Defensive Wrestler's Position

a. Hands flat on the mat and at least 8 inches in front of the knees.

b. Knees at approximately shoulder width.

c. Toes in line with the hands and knees, must not be turned in or out of the invisible plane made by the hands and knees.

PINNING COMBINATIONS

Fig. 8–9.   Front Double-Arm Bar

a. Reach with the left hand in front of defensive wrestler's left arm to his right triceps. Reach underneath his chest with the right hand and overlap your hands around his upper right arm.

b. Force his right shoulder toward mat and go around his head placing him on his back. Cross his elbows in front of his face and come out to the front, spreading your legs for balance.

Fig. 8—10. Bar-Arm and Under-hook

a. Bar the defensive wrestler's near arm with the left arm, placing the left hand on his back. Under-hook far arm with your right arm.

b. Lift with the bar-arm making sure his elbow is outside and behind the bar-arm as you step around the head with the left leg and lock hands.

c. Spread across his body being sure to keep legs apart for balance.

Fig. 8–11.   Half-Nelson and Under-hook

a. Place the left hand under defensive wrestler's left arm and up high on the head and underhook the right with your right arm.

b. Come out to the perpendicular position and put the half-nelson in deeper and force him to his back; the right arm can be placed in the crotch or around the waist.

Fig. 8–12. Straight Cradle

a. Place the left arm over defensive wrestler's head and the right arm in and behind near leg. Put the forehead in his side and attempt to lock hands.

b. Start him toward his far shoulder while raising up on his leg.

c. Stack him up while remaining on your knees and not on your side.

Variation would be to hook his free leg.

Fig. 8–13. Reverse Cradle

a. One of the best methods of working this fall is from
   the over and under ride. Lift powerfully on the far
   leg with one or both arms.

b. Take a position as close to his near hip as possible and
   sit tall. Reach around his head with the left arm as he
   is turning.

c. Collapse to his chest, flatten out, and lock hands, bringing his knee as close to his chin as possible.

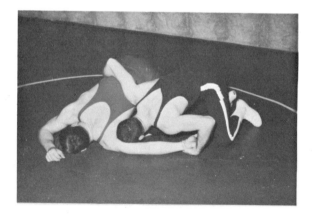

Fig. 8–14.   Head-lever Fall

a. Use a head-lever breakdown and keep the defensive wrestler's left arm straight.

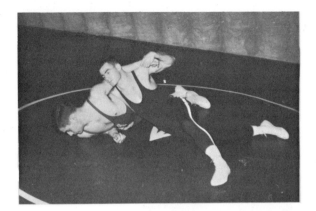

b. Lift the arm high as you sit or slide underneath. As his near shoulder reaches the upright position, release the wrist and place in a half-nelson.

c. Come out to a perpendicular position and place half-nelson deeper, pressing him to the mat.

REVERSALS

Fig. 8–15. Side-Switch

a. Move your left arm out and swing to a sit-out position, hitting on your right or outside hip.

b. Place your near arm over his arm, around and inside on the thigh.

c. Scoot hips out and away to put pressure on his shoulder, forcing it to the mat.

d. Turn toward his thigh and come up behind in a bulldog position.

Fig. 8–16.   Short Sit-out and Crawfish

a. Come out to a short sit-out position keeping control of his arm.

b. Turn in and place the left arm up and on his near thigh.

c. Shift to a position behind his hips and gain control.

Fig. 8–17. Inside Roll

a. Wing-lock the offensive wrestler's left arm; force down.

b. Step over high with the left leg and gain control by placing your right hand in between his legs in an over-and-under position with left arm reaching for a half-nelson.

Fig. 8–18.   Far-Side Roll

a. Place your hand and forearm on the offensive wrestler's arm that is around the waist.

b. Tuck in underneath with your left shoulder and fall to your far hip and elbow; this prevents exposing your back to the mat. Continue forcing him over your left side, hooking your left toe at his right knee, and lift.

c. Hit out to the perpendicular position, placing your near arm on his hip; turn toward legs for control.

BREAK-DOWNS

Fig. 8–19.   Near-Arm and Far-Instep

a. Crash his near arm at the elbow with a bar-arm hold.

b. Simultaneously grab his far instep with the other hand.

c. Drive slightly to the left.

Fig. 8–20.   Near-Arm and Bulldog

a. Crash his near arm at the elbow with a bar-arm hold.

b. Place your arm up in the rear buttock position.

c. Drive straight forward.

Fig. 8–21. Waist and Far-Instep

a. Place one arm around the defensive wrestler's waist.

b. Place the other hand on the far instep.

c. Drive straight forward.

Fig. 8–22. Head-lever and Waist

a. Slide your left hand to the defensive wrestler's near wrist.

b. Place the other arm around his waist.

c. Place your forehead in his armpit.

d. Drive forward.

RIDES

Fig. 8–23. Near-Side Ride

a. Cut or grapevine the near leg with your near leg.

b. Bar-arm the near arm.

c. Pick up the far instep.

d. Force him to the mat.

Fig. 8–24. Two-on-One Ride

a. Pick up the far instep and flatten opponent.

b. Step across bent leg, trapping with thigh.

c. Place your left arm under his near arm and grab the wrist of his far arm.

d. Reach in under his far arm with your right arm and grab the same wrist.

Fig. 8–25.   Over-and-Under Ride

a. **Place your right arm over his far thigh and reach in under his near thigh.**

b. **Pick the leg up high with either one or two arms. Sit on your knees as close to his hip as possible and keep a straight back for lifting.**

ESCAPES

Fig. 8–26. Inside-Leg Standup

a. Get altitude by lifting your chest high, grabbing the hands immediately.

b. Tuck in the near arm tightly to your body in an attempt to control his head.

c. Soon after, pop out the inside leg.

Fig. 8–27. Outside-Leg Standup

a. Get altitude by lifting your chest high, grabbing the hands immediately.

b. Tuck in the near arm tightly to your body in an attempt to control his head.

c. Soon after, pop out the outside leg.

Fig. 8–28. Tear Hands

a. **Place both hands on one of the offensive wrestler's hands.**

b. **Force powerfully down and away.**

c. **Lower center of gravity by bending at the knees.**

Fig. 8–29. Completion of Stand-up

a. **Come up with trailing leg and run out to escape.**

Fig. 8–30.   Posting Leg—Beginning position. Post the out-side leg.*

Fig. 8–31. Long Sit-Out

a. Throw the inside foot out and directly away from the offensive wrestler.

b. Maintain control of his hand.

* The moves shown in Figs. 8–30 to 8–35 can be made in four combinations: (1) short sit-out–turn-in, (2) short sit-out–turn-out, (3), long sit-out–turn-in, and (4) long sit-out–turn-out. In each combination, the wrestler finishes facing his opponent.

Fig. 8–32. Short Sit-Out

a. Slide the inside foot out and underneath your buttocks.

b. Maintain control of his wrist.

Fig. 8–33. Turn-In

a. Lift the arm from around the waist.

b. Turn toward the left elbow.

c. Lift up left arm to prevent the offensive wrestler from going behind.

Fig. 8–34.   Turn-Out

a. **Lift the arm from around the waist.**

b. **Turn toward the right elbow.**

c. **Lift up right arm to prevent the offensive wrestler from going behind.**

Fig. 8–35.   Facing Off
Completion of either the turn-in or the turn-out.

Fig. 8–36. Whizzer Hip-Drive Escape

a. Place the left arm over the right triceps of the offensive wrestler, locking it tightly to your back, and post the outside leg for balance.

b. Force down and forward on his shoulder by dropping your near hip to the mat.

c. Slide the inside leg out and through to the front, keeping pressure on his shoulder, and place the hand on his head for greater control of his movements.

KNEE TAKE-DOWNS

Fig. 8–37.   Head Snap-down

a. Set up by controlling the opponent's head and his right arm.

b. Press down and away on his head and arm, passing them laterally to the side, and continue in the opposite, left, direction; gain control with a bulldog.

Fig. 8–38. Side Drag-by

a. Take the hand that is on the opponent's head and place it on the triceps of the arm that is being controlled.

b. Guide his wrist and triceps laterally past the center of your body.

c. Continue in the opposite, left, direction and gain control with a bulldog.

Fig. 8–39. Duck-under

a. Maintain control of his head with the right arm.

b. Use the left arm to pry up on his right arm and slide the head under his armpit.

c. Continue around and gain control with a bulldog.

Fig. 8–40. Bulldog Position

Completion of head snap-down, side drag-by, and duck-under maneuvers.

STANDING TAKE-DOWNS

**Fig. 8—41.   Double-Leg Drop—
With a Trip**

a. Obtain deep penetration by
landing as close to the opponent's feet as possible and
keep a straight back, placing
the head to one side.

b. Lock the hands and trip or
back-heel one of his legs.

c. Force him to the mat, remaining back until he turns toward his stomach, to prevent the opponent from countering with under-hooks.

Fig. 8–42. Single-Leg Drop

a. Raise the opponent's right arm and step in long with the left leg.

b. Place the left arm in back of his right knee keeping the head to the inside; place the right arm on the lower front of his right leg.

c. Pick up the leg immediately, keeping head to the inside.

d. Force him to the mat by putting pressure at the knee as you spin slightly to the left.

Fig. 8–43. Duck-under

a. Set up in extended standing tie-up position.

b. On same-side duck, lift slightly on the right arm, begin sliding the head under the arm, stepping in with the left foot, trailing the right foot behind.

c. On opposite-side duck, lift the left arm, sliding the head under and stepping forward with the right leg; pull down on the left triceps while spinning to the left.

d. With the same-side duck, force down on his head while spinning to the right.

e. Pick up the near leg to assist in bringing him to the mat. Variation: Instead of going to the mat, the wrestler may choose to move into the rear standing position.

COUNTERS TO PINNING COMBINATIONS

Fig. 8–44. Counter to Half-Nelson on Stomach

Wing lock hard on offensive wrestler's half-nelson arm and turn head away, attempting to regain position on knees.

Fig. 8–45. Counter to Half-Nelson on Knees

Lift on elbow of offensive wrestler's half-nelson arm; sit through on buttocks and pivot behind opponent.

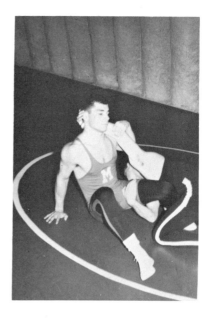

Fig. 8–46. Counter to Half-Nelson on Back

a. Bridge vigorously.

b. Drive left arm between your chest and chest of offensive wrestler.

c. Turn toward opponent.

d. Push against left leg with right hand.

Fig. 8–47. Counter to Front Double Bar-arm

a. Post right leg against the direction of pressure and attempt to force arms apart.

b. When on side, over-hook right leg, keeping parallel to offensive wrestler; force yourself back to knees.

Fig. 8–48. Counters to Straight Cradle

a. Lift head and straighten left leg.

b. Post right leg to side.

Variation: Another technique is to flatten out.

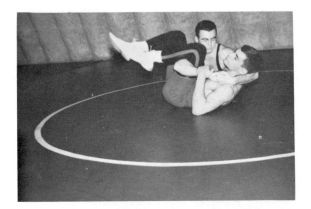

Fig. 8–49. Counter to Reverse Cradle

a. Over-hook instep of foot on cradled leg with right leg.

b. Work on offensive wrestler's hands.

c. Extend left leg and drive back with head to split hands of offensive wrestler.

COUNTERS TO REVERSALS

Fig. 8–50. Counters to Side-Switch

a. Pull near arm to his side and drive him to the mat.

**b. If unable to stop initial move, pull right arm out—
limp arm.**

c. Under-hook near leg and apply reverse cradle.

d. When switch pressure is applied on your arm, reswitch. Keep chest high, and as defensive wrestler starts behind, slide outside leg under opponent until your body is in the switch position; keep arm straight and hand on thigh.

Fig. 8–51. Counters to Far-Side Roll

a. **Sprawl away from direction of defensive wrestler's roll and loosen arm around waist.**

b. **Second move would be to jump over opponent's legs and post the right leg to stop his momentum.**

c. **Last reaction: reroll the defensive wrestler by staying parallel.**

d. **Use his momentum to roll him over your body to the starting position; lift vigorously as you execute this move.**

Fig. 8–52. Counters to Inside Roll

a. Post left leg and attempt to pull left arm free.

b. When on side, over-hook defensive wrestler's left leg
  with right leg and power up to position on knees.

A reroll technique can also be used; see far-side roll
counter.

COUNTERS TO RIDES

Fig. 8–53. Counters to Far-Instep Ride

a. Grasp wrist of hand on instep and hold while extending leg.

b. Under-hook right arm of offensive wrestler and simultaneously extend leg and lift his right arm; this move can be completed by executing a turn-in maneuver when the hand is lifted from the instep.

Fig. 8–54. Counter to Two-on-One Ride

a. **Grasp left wrist of offensive wrestler with your left hand.**

b. **Apply pressure with left hand and at same time extend and turn right hand away to break hold.**

COUNTERS TO ESCAPES

Fig. 8–55. Counters to Stand-up

a. As defensive wrestler stands, grapevine near leg with right leg and hook high on near thigh with right arm.

b. Reach left hand to back of far ankle and trip defensive wrestler by driving into the center of his body.

A variation is to place right arm around the waist and left arm in an over and under position; post left leg and use to drive into opponent.

Fig. 8–56. Counters to Sit-Out

a. Follow around with him and attempt to stay in a controlling position.

b. Drive opponent to mat and crash near arm to his side.

c. If unable to follow on a long sit-out, slide arm from around the waist to his armpit and guide defensive wrestler forward, and at the same time jump to the left and gain control; the arm guide must coincide with the time when the weight of the defensive wrestler is moving up to complete the sit-out.

COUNTERS TO KNEE TAKE-DOWNS

Fig. 8–57.   Counter to Snap-down

a. Sit through away from direction opponent is moving.

b. Pivot to knees and face opponent to remain in neutral position.

Fig. 8–58.   Counters to Side Drag-by

a. Move head to mid-line of opponent's chest and move right, remaining in head-to-head position.

b. **If unable to block initial drag-by, place right hand to triceps and execute side sit-out; guide his right elbow between the bodies in a redrag and come up behind to gain control in a bulldog position.**

COUNTERS TO STANDING TAKE-DOWNS

Fig. 8–59. Counters to Double-Leg Drop

a. Sprawl back as first reaction; flatten opponent by forcing the weight of your body on his back as legs are extended.

b. Over-hook his right arm and under-hook his left arm; pull down on over-hook and lift up on under-hook, attempting to force him to his back.

c. When opponent obtains deep penetration, use a cross-face with the left arm and bulldog with the right arm; extend legs and turn toward feet of opponent to secure control.

d. To prevent a take-down when opponent penetrates, gains control of the legs and begins to lift, reach over his back and grab both ankles.

Fig. 8–60.   Counters to Single-Leg Drop

a. Whizzer single leg arm, extend left leg, and apply pressure on right shoulder and head of opponent, attempting to move back.

b. If leg is lifted from mat, apply whizzer, control head with left hand, and place instep of right leg on the outside of his left thigh.

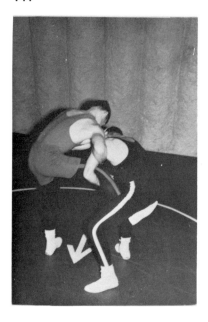

c. Another technique is to place foot between legs using same techniques as in b.

d. A jump-out maneuver can be used when unable to obtain a whizzer: As leg is lifted from mat, pivot away from opponent and vigorously pull leg free.

Fig. 8–61. Counters to Duck-under

a. Keep balanced base and hold forearm of tie-up arm perpendicular to opponent, with elbow in.

b. Wing lock arm as duck-under is executed.

c. Drop opponent's right shoulder to mat and execute inside roll.

Part III

THEORY OF COACHING WRESTLING

9

Organization and Administration

Many details must be taken into consideration in developing a varsity wrestling program. Like any project, it takes thoughtful attention to determining objectives and careful planning at all levels to achieve the best results. Often, the master of detail is the master of administration.

OBJECTIVES

The wrestling coach has a responsibility to set standards and guidelines for his program and for the young people involved. He also has a responsibility to make sure his students and his colleagues understand and support them. Of course, the coach's philosophy should be consistent with the school's educational objectives and in harmony with those of the athletic department.

The nature of wrestling gives the coach a valuable tool for helping shape the lives of young people. The coach's objectives should reflect these opportunities. One of his first objectives should be the development of human behavior. The coach should instill the spirit of competition within the framework of fair play and good sportsmanship. And while any good coach wants his boys to win and to be "scrappers" on the mat, he should also strive to develop scrappers with poise, dignity, and finesse. The coach should teach and illustrate the importance of following prescribed procedures, whether the task at hand be wrestling or any other endeavor the student undertakes. He should encourage in his charges a sense of dedication to achieving the best.

Another of his objectives must be concerned with mastering skills and developing strategy. Obviously, teaching the mastery of skills and techniques is a fundamental objective of the wrestling coach. But the coach also must recognize the importance of teaching the strategies of the sport. These strategies should be consistent with his over-all philosophy. If take-downs and escapes are of extreme importance, then a great deal of time must be spent in learning those skills. The same can be said for any other area of concentration the coach wishes to emphasize. The use of a faking maneuver for setting up your opponent is strategically sound in assessing his weaknesses or strengths during a match. Thus, the wrestler will be attempting to match his strengths against his opponent's weaknesses.

The third major objective of the coach should be concerned with enlisting the support of his program by the school, by the parents of students, and by the community. In turn, the coach should include in his objectives his cooperation and support of worthwhile school and community projects. The smart coach will encourage his students to follow this same pattern.

QUALITIES OF THE WRESTLING COACH

The wrestling coach must be enthusiastic and an aggressive worker. He must have a congenial manner and a genuine sense of humor. He needs to be an amateur psychologist to solve the many problems that will confront him, and he must be a firm disciplinarian if he is to earn and retain the respect of his wrestlers. He should never let his own professional development lag. He should become involved in local, state, and national phases of the sport, by attending clinics and tournaments, and by reading current wrestling newspapers and books. He should be proficient in demonstrating techniques and have a well-rounded knowledge of the sport.

SCHEDULING MATCHES

In most cases the scheduling of athletic contests is done through the office of the athletic director; however, the wrestling coach should be consulted. If the institution is a member of a conference, then much of the scheduling will be completed at the conference meeting of directors and coaches.

The coach should give the team an opportunity to have a reasonably successful season by winning half of the matches. This can be done by controlling the level of competition of non-conference opponents. Many coaches purposely schedule weaker teams to give themselves a chance for a "breather." This is sound practice. Going against a superior opponent week after week destroys morale and eventually harms the total program. Wrestlers deserve the opportunity to succeed while competing "in and not out of their league." Since the coach knows the relative strengths and weaknesses of his own team and should have knowledge about those of his opponents, scheduling should be a part of his responsibilities. It is good policy to have contracts made up between the competing schools with the necessary pertinent information listed.

HIRING OF OFFICIALS

Normally, the director of athletics sends out contracts on officials. The selection of the officials should be through his office, but with the assistance of the coaches of the particular sports. Because the wrestling coach is familiar with competent officials in the area, he should be given the responsibility of assigning them to the home meets.

Recognized officials of state and local associations should be used without exception if the school expects to run a sophisticated program. It should be part of the wrestling coach's responsibility to insist on good pay for an official, taking into consideration any mileage expense.

Provisions should be made for the dressing of the officials away from the normal stream of participants and spectators.

ELECTION OF CAPTAINS

The policy of selecting the captain or co-captains varies. Here are a few suggested guidelines for proper selection of the captain.

1. Have lettermen select the captain(s) from their group.
2. The coach may open the election, giving the opportunity to serve as captain to all varsity competitors, whether they are lettermen or not.
3. He may wish to make the decision himself because of the fear of having the "wrong" young man chosen.
4. Situations arise when there isn't a qualified wrestler who deserves the distinction. In this case, it is best to assign a possible leader for each of the matches in hopes that one will justify the role permanently.

The Role of the Captain

1. The captain should be the direct link between the team and the coach in all minor student personnel problems.
2. He must demonstrate the high ideals of the program.
3. He must have the respect of the group.
4. He must attempt to handle all minor problems before they become serious enough to be presented to the coach.
5. He is the leader of the drills and calisthenics during the practice and meet sessions.
6. He must be the one person who understands and is able to speak freely with the coach on any and all matters that concern the wrestling program.
7. He must be able to "fire up" the rest of the squad during match situations and at other opportune moments.

THE MANAGER'S RESPONSIBILITIES

The student manager is a very important part of the total program. He is the almost irreplaceable person who handles the myriad details that often trouble the coach. This young man can make a very positive contribution to the team.

The Role of the Manager

1. He must adhere to the rigid standards met by the varsity competitors.
2. He is responsible for the issuance of all equipment during the practice and meet sessions, when a team equipment man is unavailable.
3. He is the charter of statistics during a meet.

4. He is the coach's right-hand man.
5. He should have an understanding of the sport of wrestling. Very often a boy who can no longer wrestle because of an injury can fill the role of the manager exceptionally well.
6. He can often aid the coach in the role of assistant coach during drill situations.
7. He can also double as an assistant student trainer at home and on away meets.
8. He should be the timer and scorer of try-outs.
9. He handles the minor details of setting up a meet.
10. He should have an opportunity for winning a varsity letter.

FIRST ORGANIZED MEETING

The first meeting of the wrestling team can be very useful and beneficial. The meeting should take place in a classroom rather than in the wrestling room area, because it is a talking rather than a work-out session. All important areas should be discussed. The following are guides for structuring the session:

1. Set forth the rules and regulations which govern the behavior of the wrestlers while they are members of the program.
2. Tell the wrestlers the coach's policies and how he deals with violations of those rules and regulations; in general the policies should be consistent with those of the athletic department.
3. Explain what is to be expected during practice sessions, traveling on trips, in proper appearance and behavior; this is important for team discipline.
4. Discuss the policy on cutting a wrestler from the squad.
5. Emphasize the importance of doing well in their school work so a wrestler will not be placed on the ineligibility list.
6. Introduce team captain(s) and returning lettermen, outlining their responsibility to the program.

Miscellaneous Hand-outs

1. Prepare a mimeographed brochure on wrestling maneuvers with their description and counters, so the wrestlers will have a guide in learning the style of wrestling expected by the coach.
2. Pass out a copy of the wrestling schedule of both the varsity and junior-varsity and discuss the various teams on the schedule.

3. Parent permission slips for wrestling should be handed out to take home and be returned with signatures.

4. A medical-examination form to be signed by the family physician should be completed prior to the first organized meeting and returned at this time.

5. Equipment issuance should take place at the end of the meeting under the supervision of the manager and coach. Give equipment priority to the returning lettermen. Most coaches will have the unknown wrestlers use their own equipment until he has a chance to see them wrestle.

SET-UP OF MATS FOR DUAL MEETS AND TOURNAMENTS

Dual Meet Set-up — General Description

1. Bleachers: Have sufficient bleachers available.

2. Scorer's table: The announcer, home scorer, visiting scorer, head timer, and the two assistant timers should be at the table. Have the arrow in the center of the mat facing away from the table so the timer can see the official's signal (check NCAA *Wrestling Guide* for official ruling).

3. Warm-up mats: Place one mat behind each of the contestants' chairs for the next competitor to use while warming up.

4. Contestants' chairs: If there is only one clock (see 5a below), seat the visitors facing the clock.

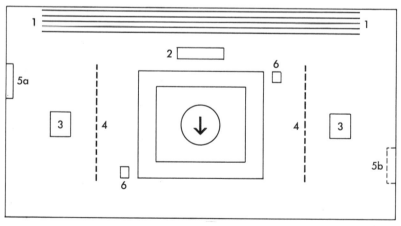

Fig. 9–1. Dual-Meet Set-up

5. Official Match Clock.

6. Foot mats: They should be situated at the spots where the contestants will enter onto the mats.

Tournament Set-up — General Description

1. Bleachers: Have all possible bleachers ready for use; have designated area for contestants.

2. Scorers' tables: (Check the NCAA *Wrestling Guide* for the official set-up of the table.)

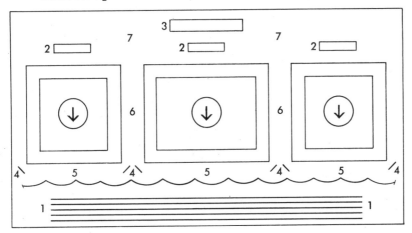

Fig. 9–2. Tournament Set-up

3. Head scorer's table: The announcer, head tournament scorer, and pairing personnel are seated at this table.

4. Coaches' chairs: Only the coaches of the contestants on the mat are allowed in the chairs.

5. Restraining rope: It is advisable to have the entire area roped off to keep unauthorized personnel out of the wrestling area.

6. Gap: It is advisable to allow some space between the wrestling areas.

7. Personnel area: Place all scorers' tables and the head scorer's table on the same side of the gymnasium to speed proceedings.

SELECTION OF THE TEAM

The selection of the varsity team can be a difficult job for the coach. Decisions made by some subjective means can be dangerous. The tryout approach, using the ladder system, is far better and more fool-proof against wrong decisions.

Once the ladder has been determined, set up a procedure which gives wrestlers an opportunity to try out for the varsity. When there are several wrestlers in each weight class, hold a small elimination tournament to decide who the number-one challenger shall be. When there are just a few in a weight class, have the challengers start at the bottom and work up to the top young man. For example, if there are three in the weight, the number-three contestant challenges the number-two contestant, and the winner challenges the top person. Situations will differ from one program to another, depending upon the number of wrestlers, but in all fairness to the wrestlers, ladder challenging is the most objective and beneficial.

The coach or his assistants should be the officials for all tryouts. This is time-consuming for the coach, but it is the only objective way. It is poor policy to place the responsibility on fellow peers, for it puts undue pressure on individual students.

It is best not to have the current varsity wrestler challenged more than once between meets. Situations arise when one continually defeats another in a tryout, but does poorly in an actual meet. If, in the coach's judgement, the defeated wrestler can do as well or maybe better, it is the coach's prerogative to hold no weekly tryout and go with the wrestler of his choice.

Another situation arises quite frequently when there are two good wrestlers in one weight class and a fair wrestler or two in a higher weight class. This is a difficult problem. Most often the coach will ask the second best wrestler at the lower weight to move up, making the team stronger in both weights.

The selection of the team depends upon the team itself; however, the coach must have the final word. Prevent difficult situations, but when they do arise the coach must make the final decision for the best interests of the team.

USE OF STATISTICS

Since wrestling is divided into six phases—standing take-downs, knee take-downs, rides and break-downs, pinning combinations, escapes, and reversals—evaluation of performance is achieved by recording the number of times each of the skills has been executed by the contestant and by the opponent during regular competition. This is a very direct approach to measurement. It quickly gives the participant a thumb-nail sketch of what he is doing well and what his opponent is doing well against him. A profile of a group of matches over a period of time gives the participant an excellent measurement of his strengths and weaknesses. These statistics, therefore, should be kept from year to year to give even a larger view of the various trends the wrestler may be experiencing from time to time.

Below is an example of a chart which may be used for recording these statistics.

INDIVIDUAL STATISTICS		
NAME _____ WEIGHT ____ OPPONENT _____		
	Standing Take-downs	
	Knee Take-downs	
	Escapes	
	Reversals	
	Near Falls	
	Predicament	
	Riding Time	
	Fall	

Fig. 9–3. Individual Statistics Chart

The statistical chart enables the participant to readily measure his apparent strengths and weaknesses in any particular phase of wrestling. Also, he will know the areas in which he must practice. This type of statistical analysis is a sophisticated approach to measurement. The participant becomes a student of the sport. Moreover, he can be constantly aware of what he is doing at any given period in the conditioning program and knows how he is progressing in each and all of the six phases.

TRAVELING WITH THE TEAM

A trip with the varsity should be a special event, regardless of the number of times an individual may have had the experience.

Being a member of the traveling squad should be an honor and distinction. The wrestlers should be dressed properly and look their best. They should have short haircuts. Their clothes need not be new but should be cleaned and pressed. Too often people assess other people by their dress and mannerisms, thus it behooves a coach to emphasize this aspect of individual development.

The importance of discipline on trips is a factor which must not be overlooked. It would be a very unfortunate and embarrassing episode for the wrestling coach to discover his wrestlers had been making a nuisance of themselves in restaurants, stores, or other public places. In a strange community, it is best to have the wrestlers in groups of three or more when they have free time.

The athletes must realize that they are in the limelight and constantly scrutinized under the pressure of the public eye. It is best to point out to them that they represent themselves, their institution, the sport of wrestling, and the coach. Explain that an embarrassing situation will affect the image of every one as well as the individual concerned.

10

In and Out of Season

THE WRESTLING SEASON

The authors have attempted to break the season of wrestling into three parts: the early season, which might have a length of five to seven weeks depending upon when the school is allowed to begin their first practice session; the mid-season, which is normally three to five weeks; and the late season, which is also three to five weeks in length. The purpose of this chapter is to familiarize the reader with the major areas of emphasis during each portion of the season. It is imperative that continuity exists from one phase to the next and that conditioning, skill acquisition, and evaluation be a continuous process.

Within each section there will be samples of daily work-outs which will give the reader a basic understanding of what is being presented. Logically, every coach will have his own variations which will be determined by personnel, experience, and facilities. However, it is the intent of the authors to formulate some general principles for sectional seasonal planning.

Early Season — Six Weeks

This portion in the wrestling season is the most important. Within these few weeks of practice, the basic skills of wrestling in each of the six phases must be presented: the skills for the escapes, rides and break-downs, knee take-downs, standing take-downs, falls, and reversals. In addition some of the countering maneuvers for each area should be covered to enable the wrestler to receive and utilize a system of wrestling skills.

The authors suggest the newer approach to the timing for presenting each of the phases. Conventional methods had the season starting with the standing take-downs; however, it is recommended that the learning of skills begin on the mat to prevent injuries which can occur in the beginning sessions due to poor physical condition and awkwardness.

To begin with pinning combinations places emphasis on the importance of remaining on the mat until conditioning is improved. This focuses attention on the fact that pinning is the ultimate objective of wrestling and therefore merits a prominent position in the teaching progression. It is recommended that the coach moves next to the reversal phase, then to the rides and break-downs, the escapes, knee take-downs, and last to standing take-downs. A major problem arises when the coach has little practice time before the first match. In this case, it would be feasible to practice the standing take-downs sooner.

With so many individual skills and variations, emphasis must be devoted to the offensive moves with some teaching of those countering techniques often associated with them. The main emphasis on the countering or defensive techniques should be covered in the next section, the mid-season.

The primary purpose of the early season is to acquire basic knowledge and skills. The secondary objective is to improve the physical condition of the team members through calisthenics, individual and dual drills, and weight lifting (see Chapter 6).

The latter part of the early season will likely include the first few matches of the schedule. One of the most important teaching techniques is to discuss each wrestler's errors and weaknesses with him following the match. This practice will help the individual to better understand and correct his weaknesses and improve upon his strengths. The best measure for evaluation is the use of the motion picture, since it gives first-hand evidence of mistakes. However, this is not always economically feasible; therefore, having the manager chart the wrestler's errors will give the coach and wrestlers a realistic means of evaluation.

SAMPLES OF EARLY-SEASON WORKOUTS—MAJOR POINTS
Daily Workout
  1. Individual and dual drills for warm-up.

2. Demonstration of reversals.
3. Execution of the reversals.
4. Execution of the basic counters.
5. Review of the basic falls.
6. Calisthenics and running.

Daily Workout
1. Individual and dual drills for warm-up.
2. Demonstration of additional reversals.
3. Execution of the reversals.
4. Execution of the basic counters.
5. One minute matches.
6. Calisthenics and weight lifting.

Daily Workout
1. Individual and dual drills for warm-up.
2. Review of all reversals.
3. Demonstration of rides and break-downs.
4. Execution of the rides and break-downs.
5. Easy wrestling using reversal techniques.
6. Calisthenics and running.

Mid-Season — Four Weeks

The most important factor in these few weeks is the emphasis placed upon the situational drill as a re-evaluating and re-educating tool for each of the wrestlers. Drills add the necessary impetus to the counter phase of wrestling. The major emphasis is on the defensive skills which are supplied during this part of the mid-season as the conditioning and over-all knowledge of the wrestlers improve.

Situational drills allow the wrestler to think under the "heat of competition" while instituting countering tactics. In these drills the execution must be performed correctly instead of just "going through the motions." Be aware of spending too great a time on drills (see Chapter 6).

Along with the situational drills, the coach should introduce the over-length match. Instead of the regulation match add a minute to each period to overload the conditioning process. Utilize the rotation system drill in which the second-string wrestler goes against the varsity wrestler in the first period, the third-string wrestler for the second period, and the fourth-string wrestler for the last period.

The series phase is often overlooked. Grouping maneuvers in a series for the purpose of emphasizing skills is an excellent teaching technique. The whizzer series with its many variations is one area to present. The front sit-out position has many skill possibilities that can be presented.

SAMPLES OF SITUATIONAL DRILLS

Double-Leg Drop Drill
  1. A drops in, B sprawls.
  2. A drops in, B sprawls, A pulls B in and trips.
  3. A drops in, B sprawls, A sits out to the side.

Snap-down Drill
  1. A snaps B, B sits out to neutral.
  2. A snaps B, B sits out to neutral, A arm drags B.
  3. A snaps B, B sits out to neutral, A arm drags B, B redrags.

Sit-out Drill—with Partner
  1. A sits out and turns in.
  2. A sits out and turns in, B follows.
  3. A sits out and turns in, B follows, A rolls.
  4. A sits out and turns in, B follows, A rolls, B rerolls.

Switch Drill
  1. A side switches, B blocks with shoulder.
  2. A side switches, B blocks, A side rolls.
  3. A side switches, B limps arm back and drives.
  4. A side switches, B reswitches.
  5. A side switches, B reswitches, A steps over.
  6. A side switches, B reswitches, A steps over, B leg lifts.

SAMPLES OF MID-SEASON DAILY WORK-OUTS—MAJOR POINTS

Daily Work-out
  1. Individual and dual drills for warm-up.
  2. Try-outs for the varsity; rest of the group, whizzer series.
  3. Take-down drills and discussion of the errors.
  4. Nine-minute matches.
  5. Calisthenics.

Daily Work-out
1. Individual and dual drills for warm-up.
2. Escape drills and discussion of the errors.
3. Front sit-out series.
4. Round-robin take-downs.
5. Calisthenics and running.

Daily Work-out
1. Individual and dual drills for warm-up.
2. Rides and break-downs and discussion of the errors.
3. Rear standing break-down series.
4. Nine-minute matches.
5. Calisthenics.

Late Season — Four Weeks

The wrestler is now reaching his peak in conditioning and skill execution. Emphasis must be placed not only on the physical preparation but also on psychological preparation. This is the time when many wrestlers come into a dangerous period for "staleness." An easy practice or a day off at strategic times is a good preventive technique.

Within this particular phase of the wrestling season, the coach must stress many forms of integrated wrestling; that is, the practice sessions should include a review of the basic techniques in each area, the situational drills, the quick-escape method, the round-robin take-down method, the two-minute wrestling period method, and many others (see Chapter 6). A combination of these methods will insure a well-rounded approach to all phases of wrestling.

The error many coaches commit is taking too much of the practice time for "full-go" wrestling. During this portion of the wrestling season, physical and psychological fatigue factors must be taken into consideration. Wrestling is unique in having its participants go through weight reduction; this factor alone can cause many of them to become physically and emotionally tired. The coach would be wise to use many short-spurt methods of conditioning and learning situations which employ short interspersed periods of rest. It would be advisable to lessen the length of the practice period occasionally, or to allow the first team to be on their own while the coach is working with the rest of the squad.

SAMPLES OF LATE-SEASON WORK-OUTS—MAJOR POINTS

Daily Work-out
1. Individual and dual drills for warm-up.
2. Fifteen-second escapes.
3. Thirty-second knee take-downs.
4. Discussion of the common errors.
5. Calisthenics.

Daily Work-out
1. Individual and dual drills for warm-up.
2. Round-robin take-downs.
3. Pinning combinations.
4. Three-minute matches with different wrestlers.
5. Running.

Daily Work-out
1. Individual and dual drills for warm-up.
2. Nine-minute matches.
3. Review of reversals.
4. Escape drills.
5. Weight lifting.

The authors wish to stress the technique of utilizing calisthenics at the end of the practice session as is shown in the brief examples of daily workouts. This approach attains maximal results from a teaching and coaching experience by having the learning session precede the calisthenic period, which is traditionally boring and fatiguing. The short individual and dual drill session will be a learning experience as well as a warm-up.

OFF-SEASON ACTIVITIES

Wrestling demands a variety of physical attributes which a champion wrestler will continually strive to improve. The dedicated wrestler will choose activities that contribute to his development even though the wrestling season might be several months away. However, the coach should also be concerned with the more typical "seasonal wrestler" who does not plan his activities with wrestling in mind once the wrestling season is completed. Through proper counseling the wrestler can be guided into activities that will benefit him from both a personal and wrestling standpoint.

Wrestlers should be encouraged to participate in other varsity sports. Other sports contribute to the psychological demands of wrestling. For instance, if a wrestler competes in track he keeps a competitive edge and should be better prepared for wrestling the next season. Qualities such as persistence and courage can be developed through participation in other sports. Wrestlers should compete in off-season sports even if only in intramural play.

Team sports have special carry-over value to the wrestling team. Even though wrestling is primarily an individual sport, a championship team is founded on principles of good teamwork.

Wrestlers also should become involved in activities which contribute to physical development. Such activities as weight lifting, gymnastics, handball, and running are excellent aids. A potential danger is that some wrestlers will over-emphasize weight lifting and its accompanying strength improvement at the expense of agility, flexibility, balance, and quickness.

Post-Season

Immediately following the wrestling season all wrestlers should be encouraged to continue some physical activity. If they do not participate in a varsity sport, the coach should make arrangements for some type of activity such as handball, basketball, or running. The wrestlers should be encouraged to maintain some degree of their physical fitness.

If a wrestler is weak in a specific area, such as agility or co-ordination, the coach should outline activities and exercises which the wrestler can practice before the next season. For instance, if a boy needs to develop better foot co-ordination, the coach might recommend a series of rope jumping exercises and participation in badminton.

Summer

During the summer months the wrestlers should seek physically demanding jobs. They need to lift weights two or three times a week and run on the evenings in between. Again, it is recommended that they participate in such physical activities as swimming and softball or baseball.

Pre-Season

The length of the pre-season period will vary three to six weeks. Most high schools are not allowed to begin practice under supervision of a coach before a designated date in November. However, the group may be conditioning on its own.

The most important phase of this session is the concern for cardio-vascular development through long distance and interval running. Prospective wrestlers who are not involved in any fall sport activity should run on a prescribed schedule. Periodically, the manager of the team will record the times for given distances to measure development.

Another phase of pre-season training is weight lifting. The weight lifting procedure suggested in Chapter 6 should be followed. If a wrestler has not lifted weights before or has not lifted since the previous season, care must be exercised so that he begins slowly and gradually builds up to a desired weight.

A third phase of conditioning consists of calisthenics and stretching exercises. The latter is a very valuable instrument that must be consistently emphasized because of the nature of the sport of wrestling. The competitor has to achieve a high level of flexibility since many wrestling skills involve twisting and turning movements.

For best results it is necessary to combine these three techniques in the most profitable but yet enjoyable set-up.

SUGGESTED FIVE-WEEK SCHEDULE FOR A PRE-SEASON PROGRAM

Session 1: Jog and walk 3 miles.
Session 2: Jog 2 miles, lift weights.
Session 3: Jog 2 miles, calisthenics, and stretching.

Session 4: Run 2 miles, lift weights.
Session 5: Run 2 miles, calisthenics, stretching.
Session 6: Jog 5 miles.
Session 7: Run 2 miles, lift weights.
Session 8: Run 8 sprints of 110 yards, calisthenics, stretching.
Session 9: Run 8 sprints of 110 yards, lift weights.
Session 10: Run 1 mile for time, calisthenics, stretching.
Session 11: Run 2 miles, lift weights.
Session 12: Run 10 sprints of 110 yards, calisthenics, stretching.
Session 13: Run 10 sprints of 110 yards, lift weights.
Session 14: Run 2 miles for time.
Session 15: Run 10 sprints of 110 yards, lift weights.
Session 16: Run 10 sprints of 110 yards, calisthenics, stretching.
Session 17: Jog 6 miles.
Session 18: First organized meeting.

11

Promotion

The efforts of the wrestling coach can't stop at the mat. He also has to be adept at recruiting a team, press agentry, salesmanship, and public relations. This chapter is an action blueprint to favorable public relations for the sport. It includes recruiting tips, publicity methods, and ideas for building recognition, status, and support. The promotional techniques presented are applicable primarily to high school wrestling, but most of them can be modified for use by the college wrestling coach.

BUILDING A TEAM

Fundamental to building a team is a coach who knows the sport, develops a program built on sound principles, and who is enthusiastic. This is the combination that makes the coach a successful recruiter and paves the way for giving status and recognition to the sport. Boys will want to try out and stay in a program that's well run by a qualified man dedicated to building a winning team.

To start a wrestling program, introduce it to students as part of the physical education program. Then, and only when skills are developed sufficiently and enthusiasm grows, add wrestling to the intramural program. The intramural program becomes the breeding ground for varsity wrestling.

If wrestling is already a part of the physical education and intramural program, here are some techniques that can help sustain the interest of the caliber of student needed for an outstanding team.

1. Hold a variety of tournaments in the intramural program, making it possible for many boys to participate.
2. Schedule different levels of competition; the total program should include freshman, sophomore, and junior varsity meets as well as varsity meets.
3. Movies, NCAA championship films, can be recruiting tools as well as teaching aids.
4. Shooting movies of team meets are helpful morale builders and useful in helping wrestlers to evaluate their own performance.
5. Set up a bulletin board for the exclusive use of the wrestling program. Devote a section to newspaper clippings, reporting results, magazine articles on wrestling, charts on techniques, team photos and photos taken at meets. Encourage students to bring in appropriate materials for posting. Don't let the board become cluttered, keep it up to date and make changes on a set schedule.
6. Display a team challenge board in a prominent place.
7. Arrange field trips which will give team members an opportunity to watch college or university wrestling teams.
8. Subscribe to a wrestling newspaper or magazine with copies available in the school library as well as in the gymnasium. Encourage team members to get their own subscriptions.
9. Develop a "rogues gallery" of past outstanding wrestlers. The photos, framed, might be hung in a section of the dressing room, or in a hallway leading to the wrestling area or gymnasium. Giving recognition to past top performers will give present wrestlers a goal.
10. Develop a rotating award or recognition program to keep team interest high. The teaching staff or a joint committee of students and faculty might select a "wrestler of the month," "top man of the meet," "most valuable player," etc.
11. Bring in outside experts to talk to the team. The speaker might be a coach of college wrestling, a physical fitness expert, or a former student active in intercollegiate wrestling.
12. Climax the season with a banquet. Include parents at this affair.

BUILDING STUDENT SUPPORT

A gymnasium full of cheering spectators can make a difference in the performance of a wrestling team, for the success of the team and the morale of its members are closely related to the backing and support of students in general. And because wrestling hasn't yet achieved the popularity and common understanding of sports like baseball, football, and basketball, it is worth the coach's effort to devote attention to educating spectators and conducting a continuous campaign to win student support.

A student committee, possibly made up of the team manager, a few varsity wrestlers, the cheerleading captain, the sports writer on the school paper, and selected student leaders, might be one approach to conducting a school-wide promotion of wrestling.

Here's a check list of publicity ideas:

1. Place schedule boards in prominent places. Make the boards distinctive to attract attention. For example, the board can be designed to look like a wrestling mat or wrestling tights.

2. Arrange for a special wrestling bulletin board in the school in addition to the one in the gymnasium area. Or, if a school-wide bulletin board is policy, make sure a section is reserved for wrestling.

3. Arrange special displays in the school cafeteria, in hallways, or even in a downtown bank. This can be done pre-season or before a major meet. Photos of the varsity members by weight classes can be the feature of the display. Life-size caricatures of the team members sketched by an art student, then constructed from heavy cardboard or plywood, is another display idea. These could be used from season to season by merely re-sketching the faces.

4. Display special announcements around the school prior to home meets. Use colored paper, or develop a special symbol that immediately identifies the sport.

5. Invite the student body or certain school clubs to a special showing of the movies taken of the team in action.

6. Put on a wrestling demonstration at school assemblies and during the half-time of basketball games.

7. Make sure the school newspaper carries wrestling news on a regular basis.

8. Organize wrestling enthusiasts into a club which attends the meets as a body. This group might also be encouraged to sponsor a "spectators' training course" for other students. Certificates might even be awarded to those who successfully learn certain basic principles. Be sure girls are included in the club.

9. Hold pep rallies before a meet and include the wrestling team when rallies are held for other sporting events.

BUILDING COMMUNITY SUPPORT

Keep in mind that citizens of a community, as parents and as taxpayers, have a vested interest in what goes on in the schools—particularly at the secondary level. Wrestling could come in for close scrutiny, because of the one-to-one combative aspect of the sport and the misconceptions created by the television brand of professional wrestling. But given a well-run program, bolstered by a nucleus of interested townspeople, wrestling can free itself of any criticisms or misunderstandings. Parents of wrestlers form that all-important nucleus.

1. Keep parents informed. Solidify parental support with pre- and post-season letters, and personal contact whenever possible. Hold a parents' night when the program's purposes and plans can be explained, misconceptions on weight control clarified, and questions answered.
2. Offer to put on wrestling demonstrations for community groups.
3. Form a parents' committee. This group could serve as liaison to the community and get support from business firms which might be willing to print schedules and flyers for distribution in the community.
4. Hold a community night before the opening of the season. Invite the mayor, members of the Board of Education, and service club presidents as special guests.
5. Seek the support of the local newspaper by providing the sports editor with regular news releases and other information.

PUBLICITY

Good newspaper, television, and radio publicity is essential if wrestling is to gain proper recognition in a locality. The coach or the sports information director provides information for this purpose.

1. Encourage your local newspaper to run a series of pre-season wrestling articles. These articles might include basic wrestling rules and technique information in an area where wrestling is new. If wrestling is established in the community, emphasis can be placed on the team prospects with stories about the individual wrestlers.

2. Keep an up-to-date set of statistics. Many news media do not publicize wrestling because the only information they receive is the score of the meet. Provide comprehensive team and individual records. The team leader in takedowns, the fastest pin of the season, and the longest dual-meet win streak are examples of newsworthy wrestling items. Provide this information after every meet.

3. Produce a wrestling brochure for use by news media and other interested people. Include the schedule; team roster, with weight class, year in school, and previous letters; past results; and record holders. Include a brief summary of prospects for the season and incorporate the individual sketches of the wrestlers and coaches. It is also good public relations to include a listing of school officials and additional information about the school.

4. Set up special events that will attract the attention of the people and be newsworthy. Ask the paper to designate a "Wrestling Week" before a particularly strong opponent or meeting a big rival. This stimulates interest and can create publicity for the team.

5. Have team and individual pictures available for speedy distribution. Take action shots at meets and use them for publicity purposes.

THE WRESTLING MEET

One of the best ways to promote wrestling is to run home meets properly and impressively. Have competent adults assist whenever possible.

1. Have a good announcer and provide him with a good loudspeaker.

2. Have music before the meet.

3. Have cheerleaders present to direct the cheering.

4. Provide a program of the participants with name, weight classification, and year in school. Provide a space for the spectator to score the meet. Include pictures if it is economically feasible. Provide some type of an informational program even if your budget will not permit an elaborate one.

5. Provide a pamphlet on "How to Watch Amateur Wrestling." This will assist the person who might not understand scoring, mat procedures, or some other phase of the wrestling meet.

6. Introduce the wrestlers on both teams prior to the start of the meet. Have the contestants at each weight cross the mat and shake hands when they are introduced.

7. Provide a visible starting line-up chart on the gymnasium wall.

8. Keep the spectators properly informed. Provide a scoreboard for individual match score and one for running meet score. Use the large wall clock to keep time for the periods.

12

Psychology of Coaching

You are fast becoming what you are going to be. . . .

Wrestling not only demands physical preparedness but psychological preparedness as well. This, unfortunately, is at times a neglected and often misdirected coaching technique. All coaches must attempt to achieve mastery in this area which is ever-increasing in importance. Let us not be naive, without the "horses" it is difficult to be a big winner; but also let us not overlook that achieving success and pursuing excellence is, as Antoine Arnauld has said, "not doing extraordinary things, but doing ordinary things extraordinarily well."

In many instances the psychological attitude of the wrestler is the single most important factor in his winning or losing. First and foremost, he must develop a psychological attitude toward competition that is conducive to the individual sport of wrestling, yet not lose the full meaning of team competition, co-operation, and spirit.

There are many ways a sophisticated program of wrestling can handle this important element which is inherent in every competitive situation. The following are a few illustrations that may be used in attempting to conquer the complex problem.

WINNING AS A MORALE BUILDER

Nothing builds a favorable attitude in competitors better than winning. Winning undoubtedly and unknowingly solves a great many problems. The competitor forgets the soreness in his foot more readily after victory than after defeat. It is important, therefore, to capitalize on winning in ways which will benefit every wrestler. Obviously some wrestlers will not be winning; therefore, make use of your winners in bolstering the attitude of the unfortunate ones. Keep wrestlers aware of the danger of overconfidence by constant evaluation of the past and future. Be careful "in slapping yourself and the wrestlers on the back." Rather, wait for the proper moment to express faith and confidence with sincere congratulatory remarks. This calls for proper insight on the part of the coach. Be sure that the individual needs the praise, but more important, be sure he deserves the praise allotted him. All wrestlers want the coach's recognition; the coach must handle this situation with extreme care. Winning is a very gratifying reality, but letting it get out of proportion is as dangerous as losing.

MAKING LOSING PROFITABLE

Losing demands the positive attention of every coach. Certainly no one likes to lose, but there has to be a loser. If losing is a frequent visitor on your doorstep, very obviously many situations have to be corrected. The attitude of the whole team may be at a low ebb. They may need a rest or change of pace. The statistics may provide clues or give a definite indication that certain drills have to be changed or different approaches made in the presentation of the various techniques or skills. Very often losing is just what the doctor ordered. It forces a wrestler to analyze his mistakes. A few undefeated wrestlers may need the scare of a close match or even a loss to bring their attitudes back into line.

MAKING WRESTLING IMPORTANT

This, fortunately, is becoming an easier and easier task for the coach because of the increased emphasis and growth of wrestling. Its growing popularity is making favorable imprints upon competitors and on-lookers. However, it is important for the wrestlers to know that their sport is major in every sense. Logically, it might not yet rank on a par with other sports, but it must be made to seem major to the competitors. This job rests primarily with the coach. Attempting to run a first-class and sophisticated program of wrestling will unquestionably gain the favor of its primary constituents. It is important to see that the wrestlers get the same treatment as the other athletes in the athletic program. This makes the wrestler truly a member of the program.

ASSESSING INDIVIDUAL ABILITIES

One of the most important factors in doing a good job of coaching is to know your personnel and know them well. When a wrestler needs correction, you must be able to assess his problems. Wrestlers want to know what they are doing wrong. Make an honest attempt to discover the problem. Being able to detect a wrestler's problem and then knowing possible solutions will give the coach a self-made evaluation of his own coaching strengths or weaknesses.

GAINING AND MAINTAINING THE RESPECT OF THE WRESTLERS

Gaining the respect of the team is by far one of the most important elements in the entire make-up of coaching psychology. Wrestlers will do a good deal more than is expected when they respect their coach and his ability. Just as in teaching in the classroom, do not attempt to disguise your limitations. If they discover a mistake, admit it readily without trying to cover it. A team will try harder, work harder, listen more intently, and have greater moments for an honest, straight-forward coach. The coach does not have to be well-liked, but it is important for him to be well-respected. A good coach does not attempt to win a popularity contest.

KNOWLEDGE OF THE WRESTLERS' BACKGROUND

The coach is better able to interpret possible inadequacies and limitations of his wrestlers when he knows and understands their family backgrounds. Having this information, he is in a better position to enhance the education of the wrestler and help solve many of the sudden and surprising problems. High school squads are very often a mixture of social and economic backgrounds. Knowledge concerning these areas will give the coach ammunition for doing a better coaching job. Serious family problems may arise which affect the behavior of a particular team member and maybe the whole squad. It behooves the coach to be aware of emergencies to help keep the program in balance.

PSYCHOLOGICAL DEVICES

This is one area that far too many coaches fail to use. Signs placed strategically around the wrestling practice area will at times have an effective psychological impact on particular team members or on the team as a whole. There are many, many appropriate sayings or slogans which meet the needs of an unusual situation. Many techniques have been used. A more recent fad is piping in music during the practice session to relieve some of the strain of monotonous routine or conversely, to attempt to "fire them up" by the fast-beating modern craze. During a dual meet the color and glamor of varsity competition is heightened by spotlight introductions and single overhead light while the match is in progress. All these and many more are attempts to "psyche up" your own wrestlers. It also makes for a first-class approach to program planning.

PRE-MEET SQUAD MEETING

Wrestling coaches do not have the opportunity to call time-outs from the sidelines. Therefore, all that can be done in building the team or an individual to a psychological peak has to be done prior to competition in the locker room or for a brief moment before each match. The type of talk depends on the personality of the coach, the situation, and the team members. If the coach is familiar with basic moves used by the opponents, it is best at this time to discuss them again briefly even though you have discussed it at length during the week. The important factor at this time is to attempt to "fire them up" for the match.

There is no clear-cut means for bringing about success in any sport activity. The athlete must want to work; he must want to compete; he must be able to punish himself; and he must want to pursue excellence both physically and psychologically. We all wish to win, and there is nothing more satisfying than winning; it keeps you going and keeps you wanting to work hard for another victory.

13

Advanced Techniques

College as well as high school squads must be continually drilled on beginning wrestling techniques which were presented in Chapter 8. However, when such skills are successfully mastered, it is important that the wrestling coach teach the advanced techniques presented in this chapter. The wrestler will continue to improve by learning additional maneuvers and by being continually challenged with their increasing complexity. Wrestling is similar to gymnastics in that there are always more advanced skills and techniques waiting for the competitor.

The authors do not attempt to present all advanced techniques. Included are the moves that are being used successfully by the leading college and high school teams in the United States. Sufficient moves are presented to give diversity to the wrestler when in a competitive situation. The wrestler who can execute a number of these moves properly has sufficient knowledge to be a champion.

Some of the counters that can be used against moves shown in this chapter are described in Chapter 8.

Even though this section deals with some elaborate maneuvers, the coach must preach the acquisition of sound basic fundamental moves for best results.

179

PINNING COMBINATIONS

Fig. 13–1.   Cross-face Cradle

a. Reach across defensive wrestler's face and place the left hand on his far triceps; place the right arm behind his right knee; force his head toward his knee with the cross-face.

b. Lock hands, roll back to your left side and over-hook his free leg.

Fig. 13–2. Partial-Stand Cradle

When defensive wrestler attempts a partial stand, throw in straight cradle; description on straight cradle is in the beginning techniques chapter.

Fig. 13–3. Split Scissors

a. Grapevine the defensive wrestler's near leg in a cross-body ride (see Fig. 13–17); reach across his back in a perpendicular position and grab his right leg.

    b. **Force him over by lifting up on the right leg; be cautious in forcing out on the legs, but instead force his right knee toward his chin and shoulders.**

Fig. 13—4. Double-Double

a. **The defensive wrestler applies a whizzer.**

b. **If he lowers his head, reach over it with your left arm.**

c. **Lock hands under far armpit.**

d. **Power him over to his back.**

Fig. 13–5. Guillotine

a. Go into a cross-body ride; take a perpendicular position across the defensive wrestler's back; reach under his right arm and place it over your head.

b. Force him to his left side, with pressure exerted on his right arm; place left arm under his head, release his right arm, and place your right arm across in front of the face.

Fig. 13–6.   Double Bar-Arm Stack

a. Bar the near arm of the defensive wrestler with your left arm; reach over and bar the far arm with your right arm and pull both together by locking hands.

b. Go around the head with the left leg, forcing him to his back; spread legs for balance.

Fig. 13–7. Spinner

a. Under-hook defensive wrestler's top arm with your right arm, putting your elbow on his back; grab his bottom wrist with your left hand.

b. Pull him back and at the same time spin around his head; place the left arm under his right armpit and the right arm in a half-nelson; force him to his back.

Fig. 13–8.   Front Whizzer

a. This position is attained as a result of a whip-over or "pancake" maneuver (see Fig. 13–33).

b. Place the left arm around the defensive wrestler's right triceps.

c. Reach across his chest and under-hook his left arm.

d. Force both arms in tightly to his body, putting pressure on his chest and sprawling the legs wide and back for balance.

REVERSALS

Fig. 13–9. Hip-Through

a. Place the left arm under the offensive wrestler's left arm and on his back; hook your left leg in and around his right leg to prevent him from countering to the left.

b. Slide your right leg through in a sit-out position, hitting on your left hip.

c. **Force your hips out and away while applying pressure with the left arm.**

d. **Throw your left leg back as you turn toward his legs to gain control.**

Fig. 13–10.   Weak-side Elevator

a. Reach underneath the offensive wrestler's near arm
   with the left arm and control his wrist with the right
   hand; place the left leg inside his thigh with the foot
   resting on his far leg.

b. Lift high on the arm and leg, scooting out the hips.

c. Power up and behind, gaining control in a bulldog situation.

Fig. 13–11.　Inside Switch

a. Post the left leg out to the side and reach in for the offensive wrestler's far thigh.

b. Hit out on the outside or left hip, placing pressure on his left shoulder (see Fig. 8–15).

Fig. 13–12.   Far-Side Roll Variation

a. Grasp the right hand of the offensive wrestler and tuck the left shoulder underneath his chest by moving the right knee in tight.

b. Force him over to his side by a quick hip rotation.

c. Turn toward the legs and gain control.

BREAK-DOWNS

Fig. 13–13.   Far-Arm and Far-Instep

a. Reach across under the defensive wrestler's chest and grab his far triceps.

b. Place the right hand on his far instep.

c. Drive toward his right shoulder.

Fig. 13–14.   Far-Arm and Bulldog

a. Reach across under the defensive wrestler's chest and grab his far triceps.

b. Place the right arm in the buttocks for a bulldog position.

c. Drive toward the right shoulder.

Fig. 13–15.   Waist and Bulldog

a. Place the left arm around the defensive wrestler's waist.

b. Reach with the right arm into the buttocks for a bulldog position.

c. Drive him forward.

Fig. 13–16.   Far-Knee and Far-Instep

a. Reach across underneath the defensive wrestler's stomach to his far knee.

b. Place the right hand on the far instep.

c. Drive toward his right side and pull.

Fig. 13–17. Cross-body Ride

a. Grapevine the defensive wrestler's near leg with the left leg.

b. Post the right leg out for balance.

c. Go across his back in a perpendicular position.

d. Grab the far ankle with either the right or both hands.

This is a beginning maneuver for many pinning combinations.

Fig. 13–18. Jacob's Ride

a. Go into a cross-body ride.

b. Swing the right leg over to the opposite side of the defensive wrestler, forcing him to his side.

c. As you step across, catch his near arm as close to the shoulder as possible and force it toward his chest.

d. Post your right arm for balance; keep your back slightly arched and elevate his leg, staying high in the thigh.

Variation would be to grab the head as you step across.

Fig. 13–19. Turk Ride

a. Place the right hand on the defensive wrestler's near thigh and lift; step across his far leg with the right leg and place your left arm under his near armpit.

b. Keep your head up and back straight and push into him with your hips, forcing him to his side; catch his left arm above the elbow, pressing it to his chest; and elevate his right leg, staying high with the foot.

Variation would be to grab the head.

Fig. 13–20. Figure-Four Scissors

a. Gain altitude and place the left leg under the defensive wrestler's stomach, locking with and behind your own right knee.

b. Place your arms under his armpits for control.

c. Drive him forward by pushing out on his arms.

Fig. 13–21. Top-Body Scissors

a. Gain altitude and throw in your legs, catching the defensive wrestler high on his thighs with the insteps of both feet; keeping the toes out.

b. Place your arms under his armpits for control and flatten him.

Fig. 13–22.   Crab Ride or Natvig Ride

a. Pull defensive wrestler back by controlling his weight with a two-on-one ride.

b. Extend your legs down the sides of his legs, placing the feet behind the knees of both of his legs, and keeping the toes up.

Fig. 13–23.   Blanket Ride

a. Climb on the back of the defensive wrestler.

b. Place a hand on each biceps, pulling him in tightly.

c. Bring both legs over his legs, keeping them to the outside for a good base.

Contact with all areas of the body is necessary for control.

Fig. 13–24. Fake Switch Step-back

a. Pop out to the side on a quick sit-out and reach in on the near thigh of the offensive wrestler's leg with the right arm (this maneuver can be used as a fake or when the opponent has blocked the switch with a strong arm) lift up your hips and begin sliding your near leg back until you turn your stomach toward the mat.

b. Pull away from the thigh and face off for an escape.

Fig. 13–25. Partial-Stand, Sit-Out, and Turn-In

a. Raise up off the knees in an attempt to stand up.

b. Pop out the near leg on an extended sit-out and move
directly away from the offensive wrestler. Begin turning in and rocking toward the right knee.

c. Come up to a face off, lifting the left arm high to prevent any counter maneuver.

KNEE TAKE-DOWNS

Fig. 13–26.   Under-arm Tilt

a. Grab up high on his right triceps with your left hand
   and lift your head up tightly in the opponent's right
   armpit. Place the right hand around his waist.

b. Or place the right hand across to far knee.

c. Force him down quickly to his right side and execute a long sit-out with the left leg, forcing him over to his right side.

d. Spin toward his legs, maintaining control over his right arm, and go into front whizzer pinning situation.

Fig. 13–27.   Front Quarter-Nelson

a. Place the right arm over the opponent's left arm in a whizzer.

b. Place the left hand on his head and come through with the right hand and lock it on your own left wrist.

c. Force down on the head and lift on the left arm in an attempt to turn the opponent over to his back.

Fig. 13–28.   Elbow Drive

a. Set up in a lock-up position on the knees. Push into the opponent with the right elbow. Pull down on his right arm with your left.

b. Twist him to his back and place his right arm along
   your left side and your right arm around his head to
   secure a pinning situation.

The opponent should be coming toward you and be off-
   balance before the maneuver is thrown.

STANDING TAKE-DOWNS

Fig. 13–29. Side-Arm Drag-by

a. Grab the opponent's right wrist with your left hand; place your right hand up high on his right triceps; guide the arm past the center of your body.

b. Step in with either leg and spin to the side; control the opponent in bulldog position or go to a rear standing situation.

Fig. 13–30. Japanese Drag

a. The opponent locks up in a regular long tie-up position with his right hand on your neck. Place your left arm over the top of his right arm and left hand behind his right ear. Grab his right elbow with your right hand and stand at an oblique angle.

b. Pull him forward with the left arm, turning your head away and passing him by as you step in behind with the left leg; go to the rear standing position.

It is best for the opponent to be coming toward you or standing still.

Fig. 13–31. Fireman's Throw

a. **Place the head under the opponent's right arm and tuck it tightly; as you step in with the right leg, grab high on his right thigh.**

b. **Sit on the left knee, keeping a straight back.**

c. Lift him up and begin turning him to the mat over your left shoulder by pushing off the posted right foot.

Fig. 13–32. Heel Picks

a. Start in an extended tie-up on the feet; you must control the head.

Take the head toward the heel for which you are reaching; this will place his weight on that foot.

b. Grab down behind the heel and force him back. Pick up the heel while he is falling.

Fig. 13–33. Whip-Over

a. Over-hook the opponent's right arm tightly with the left arm; under-hook his left arm with the right and place it up on his back; fall back and turn to the left by pulling on the over-hook.

b. Finish in a front whizzer pinning situation, spreading the legs for balance.

This maneuver can be thrown from the standing or knee position.

COUNTERS TO PINNING COMBINATIONS

Fig. 13–34.   Counter to Cross-face Cradle

a. Grasp right wrist of opponent with your left hand to prevent him from locking his hands.

b. Extend leg and straighten body.

Fig. 13–35.   Counters to Double-Double

a. Lift head to prevent half-nelson.

b. **Use hip-through action to roll opponent onto back, and break double-double grip.**

c. **If opponent releases hold and grabs your left leg, continue to scoot your hips while lifting half-nelson arm with your left hand.**

Fig. 13–36.   Counter to Guillotine

a. Drop to your right side.

b. Grab wrist of guillotine arm with your left hand.

c. Straighten guillotine arm, free your right arm, and turn
   toward your opponent.

Fig. 13–37.   Counter to Spinner

a. Pull under-hooked arm to mat.

b. Come back to base.

COUNTERS TO REVERSALS

Fig. 13–38. Counters to Hip-Through

a. Grasp far instep and drive toward near shoulder.

b. Go into Jacob's ride with arm across face.

c. Go into Jacob's ride with arm hook.

Fig. 13–39.   Counter to Inside Switch

a. Place head against stomach of defensive wrestler.

b. Place arm under far-leg.

COUNTERS TO RIDES

Fig. 13–40. Counters to Cross-body Ride

a. Catch grapevine leg of offensive wrestler with your near arm.

b. Straighten leg to prevent grapevine.

c. Bring offensive wrestler over near side by pressing on knee and dropping left shoulder toward mat.

d. Complete move by bringing your left arm over waist of the offensive wrestler to gain control.

e. **Drop to right hip as offensive wrestler inserts grapevine on left leg. Drive left elbow between the bodies.**

f. **Slide hips and come to a controlling position.**

You may finish with crossbody ride or come to a waist ride by disengaging your leg.

Fig. 13–41.   Counters to Figure-Four Scissors

a. Drop to side of figure-four lock.

b. Work arm under leg and lift; turn toward offensive wrestler.

Against an inexperienced figure-four wrestler, it is possible to bridge back into him in an attempt to gain a defensive pin.

COUNTER TO KNEE TAKE-DOWNS

Fig. 13–42. Counter to Under-arm Tilt

a. Spread legs for balance.

b. Lower hips to mat.

c. Attempt to push away and free your arm.

COUNTERS TO STANDING TAKE-DOWNS

Fig. 13—43.   Counters to Side-Arm Drag-by

a. Move head to center of opponent's body.

b. Circle free arm over opponent's back.

Fig. 13—44.   Counter to Japanese Drag

a. Step behind right leg of opponent with your left leg as you are forced forward.

b. Place left hand behind opponent's far leg.

c. Drive into opponent and go to knees for control.

Fig. 13–45. Counters to Fireman's Throw

a. Sprawl away as you feel the fireman's throw developing.

b. If caught off balance, step into opponent planting free arm for balance; attempt to attain a cross-body ride.

Fig. 13–46. Counter to Heel Pick

a. Push on right elbow of opponent to remove hand from head.

b. Slide hips away and attempt to come to your knees as you scissor right leg free.

14

Wrestling Series

The authors feel that a wrestler must be able to execute a variety of maneuvers from basic positions. If the first move does not succeed, he should be able to use a variation to complete an offensive maneuver or counter the opponent's move.

Three series groupings were chosen by the authors to illustrate the use of wrestling series in teaching and coaching. Grouping maneuvers for a method of presentation aids the student to understand and apply these skills.

The use of the whizzer and its ramifications are internationally known. Placing the whizzer in a series enables the wrestling instructor to stress the importance of this technique. As a result, the student is able to gain insight in the use of the maneuver and meet the challenge of the competitive whizzer situation.

Grouping maneuvers around the front sit-out position presents "ground" or mat techniques often characterized in the Eastern region of the United States. The twisting and turning style is prevalent among some Eastern "powers."

The rear-standing series has developed as a result of the recent emphasis on the standing-escape method predominant in the Midwestern United States.

The authors realize that other series can be developed. The type of series depends upon the philosophy of the coach and the area in which the wrestling takes place.

WHIZZER SERIES

Whizzer "Offense"

Fig. 14–1.   Whizzer Hip-Drive

a. Place the left arm over the opponent's right triceps, locking his right arm tightly to your back.

b. Post the outside leg for balance; force down on his shoulder by dropping your near hip to the mat.

c. Left leg can be elevated to aid in freeing a grapevine leg.

d. Slide the inside leg out and through to the front, keeping pressure on his shoulder; place the hand on his head for greater control of his movements.

Fig. 14–2. Whizzer to Far-Arm

a. Place the left arm in a whizzer around the opponent's right arm.

b. Reach across in front of the opponent's chest and grab the far triceps.

c. Pull forcefully on his far arm to tuck him underneath.

d. Finish in a front whizzer pinning combination.

Fig. 14–3. Whizzer to Whip-Over

a. Place the left arm in a whizzer around the opponent's right arm; power his chest up by pulling up on the whizzer.

b. **Step across with the right leg and swing the right arm across his chest under his left arm; pull down on the whizzer and continue spinning to the left.**

c. **Finish in a front whizzer pinning situation.**

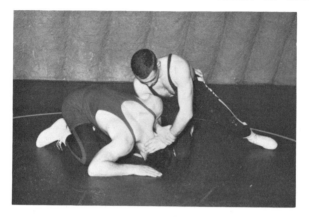

Fig. 14—4.   Whizzer to Quarter-Nelson

a. Place the right arm over the opponent's left arm in a whizzer.

b. Place the left hand on his head and come through with the right hand and lock it on your left wrist.

c. Force down on the head and lift on the left arm in an attempt to turn the opponent over to his back.

Whizzer "Defense"

Fig. 14–5. Cut-Leg and Bulldog

a. Grapevine or cut the opponent's near leg with the right leg.

b. Move the hand off the back to the buttocks in a bulldog situation.

Fig. 14–6. Sit-Back and Leg-Lift

a. Push into the opponent and step over his near leg; reach in behind the near leg with your left hand.

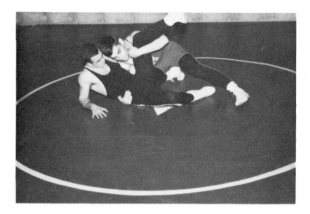

b. Continue moving to the right and lift the leg high and go behind him for control.

Be sure to force against the whizzer throughout the entire move.

Fig. 14–7. Windmill or Limp-Arm

a. Straighten out the right arm and place the palm up; move straight forward with your right shoulder to create a gap between the bodies.

b. Bring the right arm straight down close to his leg; swing the arm forcefully through to the front; move back and gain control.

Fig. 14–8. Whizzer Roll

Be sure that the opponent has thrown the whizzer maneuver before you begin the roll.

a. Tuck your left shoulder underneath the opponent's body, hitting the far knee and holding him tightly around the waist.

b. Roll under and pull him over while lifting his leg high; go toward his legs into an over and under ride, bringing your knees up for a solid base.

Fig. 14–9.   Half-Nelson

a. Come out to the side and throw a half-nelson.

b. Force him to his back by clamping down on the half-nelson and pushing him with the right arm.

Fig. 14–10.   Double-Double

a. **Come out to the side and throw a half-nelson; lock your hands under his far armpit.**

b. **Power him to his back by forcing down on the head.**

FRONT SIT-OUT SERIES

Fig. 14–11.   Basic Positions

The defensive wrestler sits directly in front of the top wrestler and keeps his body upright with hips tight to opponent.

The offensive wrestler can control the front sit-out initially with one of three hand positions while keeping pressure on his upper back.

a. The arms are placed around the waist with both hands on the midsection; they cannot be overlapped or locked.

b. Both hands are placed on the thighs.

c. One hand is placed on thigh and the other under-hooks the opposite arm.

Front Sit-Out "Offense"

Fig. 14–12.   Extended Sit-Out

a. Drive back into opponent with shoulders, and control hands around waist; attain maximum pressure by scooting hips forward.

b. Drive right arm into opponent's shoulder; complete move with turn-out maneuver.

Fig. 14–13.   Power Lift

a. Control right wrist of offensive wrestler with left hand.

b. Drive your right arm under his right arm.

c. Lift with right arm while maintaining control of wrist.

d. Turn under right arm and come to knees.

You may gain a reversal or escape.

Fig. 14–14.   Head-Pull to Either Side

a. Lock or overlap hands on head of offensive wrestler and turn toward left shoulder; pull wrestler over shoulder and come to your knees.

b. Repeat procedure number one except turn to your right.

Fig. 14–15. Side Drag-by

a. Hook offensive wrestler's triceps with right hand; scoot
   out and away.

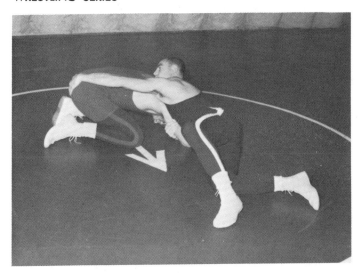

b. Turn toward the opponent by scissoring your legs; reach
   for bulldog position and gain control.

Fig. 14–16.   Granby Roll

a. Drop to left side, keeping legs clear of offensive wrestler.

b. Come to knees and turn toward top wrestler; place left arm between legs and hook his left leg.

c. Roll him over your back.

    d. Grab right wrist of opponent with left hand, and then shift right arm around his neck; lift on leg and tilt shoulders toward mat.

It is best to lock the hands for control.

Front Sit-Out "Defense"

Fig. 14–17.   Straight Drive

a. Destroy arm brace of defensive wrestler by pulling him to side.

b. Drive him onto his side.

Fig. 14–18.   Suck-back

a. As the defensive wrestler moves to the front sit-out position, shift your left hand to his chin; under-hook with the right hand.

   b. Move to an oblique angle and simultaneously suck
      shoulders of defensive wrestler to mat; place head over
      his right arm and keep a tight grip on chin.

Fig. 14–19. Crowd and Side-Tilt

a. Keep right hand on right
   thigh of defensive wrestler;
   place left hand under left
   knee and crowd him.

    b. **Move to left side and tilt defensive wrestler to his right side.**

Fig. 14–20. Cross-face Cradle

a. **Go over left arm of defensive wrestler and grasp his right triceps with your left hand; bring your right hand under his right leg.**

b. Grab your own wrist, keeping defensive wrestler's triceps, and scoot aside, dropping his back to the mat; hook far leg with your right leg and force your stomach toward mat.

Fig. 14–21.   Reverse Cradle

a. Press forward on defensive wrestler's back, jumping out to side; place right arm around his neck and left arm behind his left knee; lock hands.

b. Drop his back to the mat and over-hook his free leg.

Fig. 14–22. Spin to Front

a. Apply pressure on back of defensive wrestler; attempt-
    ing to lower his head; begin spinning to front, leading
    with left leg, and grab far leg with left hand.

b. Place knees inside legs of opponent; lift with hands placed under knees to force back to the mat.

REAR STANDING SERIES

Rear Standing "Offense"

Fig. 14–23. Tear Hands

a. Place both hands on one of the offensive wrestler's hands.

b. Force powerfully down and away with both hands in order to break the lock.

c. Lower the center of gravity by bending at the knees.

d. Run out for the escape.

Fig. 14–24. Step-back

a. Place the left leg behind the offensive wrestler's right leg.

b. Squat down and reach in between his legs with the left arm.

c. Force him straight back to his buttocks with use of the posted right leg.

Fig. 14–25. Spike

a. Bust out to the front as the lock is broken; control the one hand and lean back to force the offensive wrestler away; raise the right arm up and over his head.

b. Spin rapidly to the right and at the same time scissor legs by shooting the right leg straight back; force off, lowering the center of gravity, and control his arms.

Fig. 14–26. Standing Switch

a. Maintain control of the defensive wrestler's hands; walk straight forward to create the gap between the bodies.

b. Fall forward, landing on the right hand.

    c. Sit out to the left side and place the left hand on his right thigh; apply pressure on the shoulder to complete the switch.

Rear Standing "Defense"

Fig. 14–27. Cut-Leg or Front-Trip

a. Crowd the left side as tightly as possible; step in front of the defensive wrestler's left leg.

b. Force him straight to the mat; release your left arm and post it out to the side.

Fig. 14–28. Back-Knee Spin-Down

a. Place the right foot behind the defensive wrestler's right knee and collapse his leg.

b. Pull him tightly back and to the right side, being careful not to create a gap between the bodies; fall to the right and come up behind with the left knee high in his buttocks.

Fig. 14–29. Back-Heel

a. Place the left foot in back of the defensive wrestler's left heel.

b. Place the right knee up high in his buttocks.

c. Spin tightly to the left, being careful not to create any gap between the bodies; come up with the right knee remaining in the buttocks.

Fig. 14–30. Shoulder-Buck

a. At an opportune moment, release the lock of the hands.

b. Drop to your knees, placing your hands at his shoe laces.

c. Place the right shoulder at a point higher than the back of his knees.

d. Buck him straight forward and at the same time pull back on his feet.

Fig. 14–31. Horizontal-Lift and Trip

a. Pick the defensive wrestler straight up in the air.

b. Kick the left lower leg with your left foot.

c. Turn him slightly to the left while in the air and bring him safely to the mat on his left side under control.

Glossary

Bad Points. Points received by wrestlers in international scoring procedures. Six bad points eliminates the contestant.

Black Mark. (See bad points.)

Block. A move that stops an opponent's initial move attempt.

Body Slam. After lifting an opponent off the mat, bringing him back to the mat with unnecessary roughness.

Break-down. Destroying the base of the defensive wrestler so that he is brought flat on the mat.

Bridge. Holding shoulders off the mat by keeping weight on the head and feet.

Catch-as-catch-can. Style of wrestling used by the colleges and high schools which allows holds above and below the waist and use of legs in an effort to secure the control or achieve a fall.

Cauliflower Ear. An ear disfigured by fluid accumulation under the skin of the ear due to external pressure.

Chain Wrestling. Continuous wrestling whereby wrestlers execute a series of moves, each being determined by the previous maneuver of the opponent.

Counter. A retaliatory move executed to neutralize an opponent's action while maintaining or gaining control.

Decision. The awarding of a match to the wrestler with the most individual points when a fall has not occurred.

Default. When one of the wrestlers is unable to continue due to an injury.

Defensive Wrestler. The wrestler who is in the bottom position on the mat.

Escape. The defensive wrestler gains a neutral position.

Fall. Any part of both shoulders or area of both scapulas are held in contact with the mat for two seconds (one second in college).

Far Side. The side of the defensive wrestler away from the wrestler who is in the offensive referee's position.

Forfeit. When a wrestler does not appear for the match.

Freestyle. See Catch-as-catch-can.

GRECO-ROMAN. Style of wrestling which does not permit holds below the hips or use of legs for gripping, pushing, or pressure.

HEADGEAR. A protective device worn by wrestlers to prevent injury to the ear.

ILLEGAL HOLDS. Techniques which are not allowed because of possible danger to the participant (see Chapter 2).

LEG WRESTLING. A style of wrestling which emphasizes the use of the legs in controlling and pinning an opponent.

NEAR FALL. A position in which the offensive wrestler has control of his opponent in a pinning situation with both shoulders or the scapula area held in contact with the mat for one second (less than one second in college), or when one shoulder of the defensive wrestler is touching the mat and the other shoulder is held within one inch or less of the mat for two full seconds.

NEAR SIDE. The side of the defensive wrestler which is closest to the offensive wrestler in the referee's position.

NEUTRAL POSITION. Neither wrestler has control.

OFFENSIVE WRESTLER. The wrestler who is in the top position on the mat.

OVERTIGHTS. Close-fitting shorts worn over long tights.

OVERTIME. Extra periods wrestled in tournament competition in order to determine a winner when the regular match ended in a tie.

PENALTY POINT. Point awarded for any infraction of the rules by the wrestler.

POSITION OF ADVANTAGE. A position in which a wrestler is in control of his opponent.

PREDICAMENT. A position in which the offensive wrestler has control of his opponent in a pinning situation and a fall or near fall is imminent. A predicament occurs when both shoulders of the defensive wrestler are held momentarily within approximately four inches of the mat or less or when one shoulder is held at an angle of 45 degrees or less with the mat.

REFEREE'S POSITION. The starting position assumed by both wrestlers to begin the second and third periods and the position assumed any time the wrestlers are brought to the center of the mat after going out-of-bounds with one wrestler in control. The down wrestler is in the defensive position and the top wrestler is in the offensive position.

REVERSAL. The defensive wrestler gains an offensive position.

RIDING. When the offensive wrestler is in control of the defensive wrestler.

STALEMATE. When neither wrestler can improve his position and a pinning situation is not present.

TAKE-DOWN. A contestant brings his opponent to the mat and gains control.

TIGHTS. A part of the official wrestling uniform that covers the legs.

TIME ADVANTAGE. The wrestler in control receives "riding time" throughout the match. At the end of the match the wrestler who has one minute in excess of his opponent receives one point; if he has two or more minutes in excess of his opponent then two points are awarded. No more than two points may be awarded in any regular match.

Bibliography

Books

ARMBRUSTER, DAVID A., et. al. *Basic Skills in Sports for Men and Women.* St. Louis: The C. V. Mosby Company, 1963.

BROWN, ROBERT L., and D. KENNETH OBER. *Complete Book of High School Wrestling.* Englewood Cliffs, N.J.: Prentice-Hall, Inc., 1962.

DRATZ, JOHN P., MANLY JOHNSON, and TERRY McCANN. *Winning Wrestling.* Englewood Cliffs, N.J.: Prentice-Hall, Inc., 1966.

FAIT, HOLLIS F., et. al. *A Manual of Physical Education Activities.* Philadelphia: W. B. Saunders Company, 1961.

GALLAGHER, E. C., and REX PEERY. *Wrestling.* New York: The Ronald Press Company, 1951.

GARDNER, FRANK "SPRIG." *Wrestling.* New York: Thomas Nelson and Sons, 1963.

HUNT, M. BRIGGS. *Greco-Roman Wrestling.* New York: The Ronald Press Company, 1964.

KAPRAL, FRANK. *Championship Wrestling.* Englewood Cliffs, N.J.: Prentice-Hall, Inc., 1964.

KEEN, CLIFF, CHARLES SPEIDAL, and RAY SWARTZ. *Championship Wrestling.* Annapolis, Maryland: U.S. Naval Institute, 1964.

KENNEY, HAROLD, and GLENN LAW. *Wrestling.* New York: McGraw-Hill Company, 1952.

MACIAS, RUMMY. *Learning How . . . Wrestling.* Mankato, Minnesota: Creative Educational Society, 1964.

MARTIN, GEORGE. *The Mechanics of Wrestling.* Madison, Wisconsin: College Printing and Typing Company, 1962.

SASAHARA, SHOZO. *Scientific Approach to Wrestling.* Japan: Chuo University Co-operation Press, 1960.

SEATON, DON CASH, et. al. *Physical Education Handbook.* Englewood Cliffs, N.J.: Prentice-Hall, Inc., 1965.

SPARKS, RAYMOND. *Wrestling Illustrated.* New York: The Ronald Press Company, 1960.

UMBACH, ARNOLD, and WARREN JOHNSON. *Successful Wrestling.* Dubuque, Iowa: William C. Brown Company, 1960.

Periodicals, Guides, and Pamphlets

A.A.U. Wrestling Guide. Free style and Greco-Roman Rules. Published yearly by the Amateur Athletic Union of the U.S.A., New York, New York.

Amateur Wrestling News. Editor: Jess Hoke. Oklahoma City, Oklahoma. Published 16 times a year. Contains results of amateur wrestling meets and tournaments, articles of interest to wrestling enthusiasts, and is considered to be the voice of amateur wrestling in the United States.

NCAA Wrestling Guide. The Official Rules Book and Record Book of Collegiate and Scholastic Wrestling. Published yearly by the National Collegiate Athletic Association, New York, New York.

RASCH, PHILIP, and WARREN KROLL. *What Research Tells the Coach About Wrestling.* Washington, D.C. American Association for Health, Physical Education and Recreation, 1964.

Scholastic Wrestling News. Colorado Springs, Colorado. Published 16 times a year. Devoted exclusively to schoolboy wrestling.

Wrestling Aids and General Information

Extension of Wrestling Committee of the NCAA Wrestling Coaches and Officials Association. This committee provides wrestling information and material free of charge to those who request it.

RASCH, PHILIP J. "Bibliography of Thesis and Dissertations on Wrestling," *Journal of the Association for Physical and Mental Rehabilitation,* 16:1, 20–23. Jan.–Feb. 1962.

Films and Filmstrips

Arizona State University Wrestling. Premier Wrestling Products, Sunbury, Pennsylvania.

Beginning Wrestling. Five color filmstrips. Champions on Film, Ann Arbor, Michigan.

Championship Wrestling on Film. Cliff Keen, Ann Arbor, Michigan; or Harold Nichols, Ames, Iowa.

Maneuvers Essential for Effective Wrestling. Raymond E. Sparks, Springfield, Massachusetts.

National Collegiate Athletic Association Championships. Filmed each year. NCAA Film Service, Chicago, Illinois.

Ready Wrestle. Illinois Bell Telephone Company, Chicago, Illinois.

Wrestling: Basic Skills. John Colburn Associates, Inc., Wilmette, Illinois.

Wrestling Fundamentals and Techniques. Audio-Visual Center, University of Michigan, Ann Arbor, Michigan.

Wrestling Loop Films. The Athletic Institute, Chicago, Illinois.

Index